FOREVER SUNDAY

FOREVER SUNDAY

A Mother-Daughter Memoir

SUSAN MORLEY

CONTENTS

Dedication	vii
INTRODUCTION	1
I **THE FUNERAL**	**3**
1 Her Purse	5
2 The Gathering	8
II **HER STORY**	**11**
3 Growing Up on the Ranch	13
4 Holidays	26
5 Finding Her Path	29
6 Military Life	32
III **MY STORY**	**37**
7 My Childhood	39

8	Pirmasens, Germany	53
9	El Paso, Texas	70
10	Susanville, California	76
11	Red Bluff, California	85
12	Sacramento, California	92
13	Heaven or Hell	133
14	Another Mistake	138
15	Finally Getting it Right	143
16	A Long Story Short	146
17	My Father's Passing	149
18	Changing Times	155

IV
A SLOW GOODBYE — 173

19	Losing Her Memory	175
20	In the Hospital Before Diagnosis	187
21	After Diagnosis	190
22	Her Final Days	218

Acknowledgments — 223
About The Author — 224

In memory of my mother

Copyright © 2021 by Susan Morley

All rights reserved.

No part of this book may be reproduced in any manner whatsoever without written permission except in the case of brief quotations embodied in critical articles and reviews.

FOREVER SUNDAY is a work of nonfiction. Some of the names of the individuals featured throughout this book have been changed to protect their privacy.

From THERE'S A HOLE IN MY SIDEWALK: THE ROMANCE OF SELF-DISCOVERY by Portia Nelson. Copyright © 1993 by Portia Nelson. Reprinted with the permission of Beyond Words/Atria Books, a division of Simon & Schuster, Inc. All rights reserved.

ISBN 978-1-7363292-0-7 (hardcover)
ISBN 978-1-7363292-1-4 (ebook)

Cover design by Michael Rehder

Unless otherwise noted, all images are courtesy of a private collection.

www.susanmorley-author.com

Printed in the United States of America.

First Edition, 2021

INTRODUCTION

When my mother died in 2013, I started formulating this book even though I realized the window I'd had to ask her questions had forever closed. There is a cruel finality with death. There are no more opportunities to ask questions, no more opportunities to call and say hello, and no more opportunities to go for a visit. Years before she passed, I had the privilege of interviewing her for a women's history class I was taking. I developed most of my stories about her childhood from this interview and the stories she shared with me over the years. This book not only portrays my mother's life, but also a large part of my life. It reaches across a span of time beginning when my mother was born, in 1917, and ending with her passing in 2013—96 years.

My mother was born in a time when the world literacy rate was about 23%, a time when it took three months to travel from London to New York by ship, a time when only 8% of the population had telephones, and a time when the horse and buggy were just as common a sight as automobiles. I'm attempting to offer a glimpse of what life was like throughout this history of time and portray a relationship between a mother and her daughter.

I'm writing this book for my children, for my grandchildren, and for future generations so they will discover a part of our family history that might have been lost otherwise. I would have loved to have read a book written by my grandmother or great-grandmother, and that is what perpetually nagged at me and propelled me to write this book.

I'm also writing this book for anybody who has had, or is still dealing with, a loved one with Alzheimer's disease. This disease is horrific, and those with a loved one in its clutches know the frustration and guilt associated with it. I would also like to draw attention to some of the warning signs of Alzheimer's, signs that my mother's health care workers and we, her well-meaning family, sadly missed. I'd like to answer questions about Alzheimer's disease that would have helped us understand what was happening to my mother earlier.

I have dug down deep inside myself to write a book that is truthful, genuine, and heartfelt. I wrote about events that were integral to my relationship with my mother, that I thought I had locked away and would never share, but in the end I decided they are a huge part of who I am and reveal why I am the person I am today. I therefore couldn't, if I were to be honest with myself, leave those details out. Writing this book has been incredibly cathartic and therapeutic for me. Writing granted me the opportunity to see the world through my mother's eyes, and for that reason I'm grateful that I can now look back and see my mother for who she was.

This book covers the beginning of my mother's early life, parts of my life, how our relationship developed, and the ways in which it changed when Alzheimer's disease struck.

PART I

THE FUNERAL

"Hello?" I answer the phone.
"Susan?"
"Hi, Mom."
"How are you this evening?" my mother asks.
"Tired. I had a long day at work. How was your day?"
"Well, some religious group came to the door this afternoon and your dad invited them in," she retorts.
"Why did he do that?" I ask.
"I don't know, you know how he is. He loves a good debate."
"Well, I guess it's better he pick an argument with them than you."
"I guess," she admits. "They stayed for over an hour."
"I can imagine. What did you do during all this?"
"I sat and watched."
"Did you offer them something to eat or drink?"
"No."
"They might have stayed longer if you had," I tease.
"That's why I didn't. I could not wait until they left. I could have killed your father!"

CHAPTER 1

Her Purse

* * *

She looked beautiful and serene: her short, full-bodied silver hair beautifully styled. Her large, signature leather purse neatly tucked beside her. Her pale blue eyes closed as though she were asleep. I sat in a pew with the funeral director, feeling drained. Offhandedly, I mentioned that whoever styled my mother's hair had done an incredible job. He excused himself for a minute, returned, and quietly seated himself next to me again. He had been eager to relay my compliments to the women who had worked on her, since they didn't often get compliments.

My mother had instructed me to arrange her funeral much like the one we had for my father. She'd detailed step-by-step what she thought a proper funeral entailed. She'd wanted a viewing of her body the day before the service. The next day would be the funeral, where all her friends and family would gather to share our heart-rending grief, as we gazed at her lifeless but dignified body in a beautiful open casket before us. Immediately following the funeral, there was to be a graveside service.

And that is exactly the funeral she had.

She would have loved her funeral, which was packed with friends from all eras of her life. As music softly played in the background, people crowded into the funeral parlor, trying to find a place to sit in the packed room. Many who came to pay their respects were left standing in the back. I was pleased to see such a turnout. She had her friends from her church, bowling team, neighbors, and some friends of mine. Looking around, I realized she had outlived most of her good friends.

I sat in the special pew reserved for family, alongside my husband Sam, my children Rebekah, Matt, and Amanda, and my brother Jim, with their respective families. Jim and I are my mother's only two children.

Jim and his family lived over 80 miles away, and they usually visited my mother on special occasions and holidays. Sometimes, he came alone, to help her with projects around the house or just to visit. My children, by this time, were adults and had their own relationship with her. They loved the family gatherings at her home, eating her famous chili and sitting around the kitchen table bantering with each other. The memories of those times were our comfort as she started losing awareness of those she loved, long before she passed.

When everyone had found a place to settle, my mother's pastor got up and said a few words, with an inspirational "surrendering to God" message. I had picked out a couple of poignant religious songs that I knew were her favorites, for two of her friends to sing. At one point in the service we presented a slide show of my mother's life, which Sam had judiciously put together. There was a video placed in one section of the slide show that came to life and we saw my mother laughing while pointing her finger in a lecturing manner.

Some of the pictures portrayed her as a young mother with her husband and children, bowling as a young woman, or sitting at a slot machine gambling. Her church disapproved of gambling, but my mother wasn't one to be bothered with rules.

There were also pictures of her after being diagnosed with Alzheimer's disease. She had that blank look that develops when the mind falters. After the slide show, it was profoundly quiet, apart from sniffles, rustling of tissue paper, and blowing of noses. I stood up and said a few words, revealing to the audience the meaning of the leather purse beside her body.

"Thank you for coming today. I know my mom would be pleased. I want to explain why I placed her purse in the coffin next to her. Her purse was her identity. She never went anywhere without that purse and even when she ended up in the hospital with pneumonia, she slept with it by her side. There were times she forgot who I was, but she never forgot her purse. Inside the purse I put the cover of her checkbook and a little New Testament Bible that had belonged to my father. I thought it appropriate to bury her with them."

After I sat down, many of her friends stood up and reminisced about the good times they had spent with her. A common theme running through all the tributes paid to my mother was that she had spunk. I couldn't help but notice, and be amused, that nobody described her as being sweet. There was laughter and some bantering, and then it was over.

CHAPTER 2

The Gathering

"I kind of wanted to talk to you, Susan. No hurry, nothing really important. I just wanted to visit a little bit with you. I'll talk at you another day. Bye."

* * *

The director ushered the people out of the parlor for the graveside service. He left our immediate family alone so we could have a final moment to say our goodbyes. We then went to a covered site where my mother's body would be buried next to my father's. We were on a hill in the cemetery reserved for veterans, honoring my father's career of 20 years with the Army. It was a beautiful May afternoon, the warm breeze starting to slightly kick up. Luckily, it was before the Sacramento Valley's stifling heat had settled in with all its force. My mother's pastor stood and solemnly spoke something about her soul being in a peaceful place and then he said a prayer. I stood and looked aloofly down into the empty pit as they lowered the coffin into the grave.

Some of her friends invited us to the church to eat sandwiches and salads. When we got there, we sat down at a table reserved for family. We didn't particularly like some of the people in this church and were only there out of an obligatory respect for my mother. The pastor's wife came over to tell me how I reminded her of my mother and the regal way she presented herself, which I took as a compliment. My mother's friends took turns stopping and talking to us as we nibbled our food. When we finished eating and were ready to leave, we could put this day behind us. I finally had closure.

I breathed a sigh of relief when we got into the car to go home. I needed time alone to grieve that she would no longer be in my life. The finality that I would never be able to see her or hear her voice again was heartbreaking.

Caring for her as she struggled with her memory and emotional distress had been exhausting. It had been a long and horrific nightmare dealing with my mother as she was claimed by Alzheimer's. There was an ache in my stomach, and I knew that I needed to process my thoughts on all that had happened during this time.

PART II

HER STORY

I'm talking to a friend on the phone when call waiting interrupts.
"Hold on a minute," I say to my friend.
"Hello?"
"Susan? This is Mom."
"Hi Mom, can I call you right back? I'm on the other line talking to a friend."
"Oh, okay. Call me back." She hangs up.
Within a minute I'm interrupted again.
"Hello?"
"Susan? This is Mom."
"Mom, I'm still talking to my friend. I'll call you right back."
I flip over to the line my friend is on.
"That was my mom again."
Within a minute I'm interrupted again.
"You've got to be kidding me. What has gotten into my mother!" I say to my friend. "Just a minute."
"Susan? This is Mom."
"Mom, why do you keep calling me? I'll call you right back," I exasperatedly exclaim.

CHAPTER 3

Growing Up on the Ranch

* * *

My mother grew up on a ranch in Cambridge, Kansas. I went there once with her when I was a young girl because she wanted to revisit the house she grew up in. Her parents had died years before in an automobile accident, and she hadn't visited since her brother, taking advantage of the disarray following their sudden deaths, had seized the house and property.

As we neared the property, I could tell she was upset because her brother had let the house deteriorate. I stood in shock, staring at the old, dilapidated house that had once been her home. Obviously abandoned for years, the house seemed desolate amidst the surrounding serenity of honey-colored fields. The small house looked modest and unassuming, the wood it was built from was weathered, and beaten with years of neglect. The weeds stood tall and threatening near the doorway, as if to say, *I dare you to come near.* It was hard to imagine a loving, happy family ever living there.

When my mother's memory was fading, she illustrated with her hands the size of the foundation stones they used, which, according to her, were 18 inches long and 8 inches high. In its early stages, Alzheimer's affects short-term memory. Normally, however, as the disease progresses, long-term memory is also affected. It amazed me to think that at times when she couldn't remember who I was, she could still remember this minute detail.

We walked up close to the house and stood outside for some time. I tried not to fidget, standing beside her as quietly as I could. I closed my eyes and felt the warm summer breeze gently swirling around us. A loud creaking noise startled me, and I realized my mother was struggling to open the door. We crept inside, with me slightly hesitating behind her. While our eyes adjusted to the dark, I crinkled my nose, immediately whiffing something old and musty. I couldn't tell which room had been the living room or kitchen, but she knew. I saw the look of melancholy in her eyes, even though I didn't yet fully understand the impact of what this house had meant to her. We stayed much longer than I was comfortable with, but I silently remained by her side. Something inside me knew this was an important moment for her.

After going through the entire house, we went back outside, and my mother suggested we take a walk. I don't remember how long we walked or how far the property stretched; I was content to be out in the fresh air. My mother loved "walking the property," as she called it. So together we reverently strolled around the entire perimeter of the estate. I thought I heard her speak, so faintly I wasn't sure if she was speaking to me or just talking to herself. I cocked my ear and held my breath so I could hear her more clearly.

In a soft voice I could barely hear, she said she was a water witch. She started describing how she would find the perfect Y-shaped twig, holding the long end so the Y pointed toward the ground. She would walk around until she could feel a vibration, which grew stronger as she approached a large quantity of underground water. She was proud that the neighbors used her, or people like her, to find the best location to dig their wells. Even though I was young, I was fascinated with this revelation and accepted what she told me without question. After walking the property, we got back into the car and sat until she finally started the car and drove away.

On the way back to meet my father and brother, my mother cheered up and told me some of her childhood memories. She revealed to me that she'd had a happy childhood and felt fortunate to have had such wonderful parents. As she fondly spoke about her parents, my mother had a melancholy look, and I listened with interest.

Later in life, I received an oral history from my mother that had been passed down through several generations, along with some written articles that I found in my mother's personal files. Although my mother didn't share all of it that day in the car, it feels right to include some of the additional information here because I can see how the extended family shaped who my mother, and then I, became.

My mother's paternal grandfather, John Walter Hillier, was born in Somersetshire, England in 1847. He came to America at the age of 23, and settled in Rock Creek, Ashtabula County, Ohio. Two years later, her grandmother, Annie Jamima Davis who was born in Birmingham, England in 1845, came to America to join him.

Annie, affectionately known as Amos, stood 4 feet, 2 inches tall and weighed less than 100 pounds. She claimed to have been left at Queen Victoria's door and raised by the queen. My mother insisted this was true even though I never found evidence of this. My mother also claimed that Amos might have been the illegitimate child of one of the queen's children. As the story goes, Amos grew up as the queen's personal lady-in-waiting, which entailed helping the queen with her wardrobe and singing for her entertainment. My mother's grandfather John was supposedly the footman for Prince Albert.

Annie traveled third class on the bottom level of the ship. She was only allowed to bring her clothes, basic provisions for the trip, and a Bible or other family heirlooms. For these special items, she selected a clock and her wedding dress, which she claimed the queen provided for her. She knew that primitive living conditions on the lower deck of the ship would make traveling difficult, and she was right. There was limited space and no privacy. The passengers slept in narrow bunks and dealt with the stench of vomit from seasickness and unemptied chamber pots. They weren't allowed outside during storms, and when the weather was rough, they slid around the cabin, nearly unable to stand. Typhus, cholera, and dysentery were rampant, and many didn't survive the trip. Amos considered herself fortunate because for the most part the weather was good. The crossing took 21 days.

John and Amos were married once Amos arrived. They bought a team of horses and a wagon and headed west. The trip was long and arduous. Typically, wagon trains averaged 10 miles a day, taking many months to reach their destination depending on weather, roadway conditions, and health of the travelers. John and Amos traveled during the summer, and spent the winter in a log cabin that they built themselves. Their son Walter, my mother's father, was born in Ohio.

They lived in northern Ohio for nine years until they moved their family to Kansas in 1880. They were the parents of six daughters, Alice, Edith, Flora, Mabel, Lydia, and Ada May, and two sons, Fred and Walter. John homesteaded a claim of prairie land near the schoolhouse located in Windsor, three miles east of Cambridge, a cattle-shipping town with a restaurant and hotel. For several years he farmed corn. Their neighbors held them in high esteem. They moved to Cambridge, leaving Walter to manage the farm, when John retired.

My mother was six years old when her Grandfather John died in 1923. She remembered him stretched out on the bed at her grandparents' house, looking very distinguished with his handlebar mustache and two silver dollars laid carefully over each eye. Back then, the women laid out the dead, while the men built pine box coffins and buried them. Walter inherited the ranch, since Amos lived in town. She never remarried nor, to my mother's knowledge, was involved with any man after her husband's death. She lived by herself and managed her own affairs until she died in 1936 at the age of 91. It was never known where she got the money to live; however, it was rumored that money came from England for her support. Since my mother was 19 when her grandmother died, she had many happy memories of holidays and lazy afternoons.

Lillie Mae Ledgerwood, my mother's mother, was also of English descent; her grandparents had emigrated to America from England. Lillie Mae's mother, my mother's grandmother, Frances Marr Sarah Ledgerwood, died in childbirth in 1899 at the age of 37. The baby, a son, was raised by Lillie Mae's paternal aunt. Lillie Mae, at the age of 18, raised her other siblings—five girls and three boys. She made sure all the children graduated high school because that was her mother's dream. The boys inherited land and became farmers. The girls became seamstresses, an acceptable profession for women, and interestingly, not one of Lillie Mae's sisters bore children of her own, opting instead to adopt.

Lillie Mae and one of her sisters went on to college. Lillie Mae went to St. John's School of Nursing and became a nurse, and her sister went to a private business school and eventually worked as a "Harvey Girl," managing a Harvey House restaurant along the train line. Because trains didn't serve food in those days, and the areas around the stations were still unsettled, these restaurants were important pit stops, where travelers could rely on good food and friendly service.

Lillie Mae was satisfied with her career and her life as an independent woman. Though she was reluctant in some ways to marry Walter because it meant giving up her career to raise children, they did marry. Lillie Mae was not one to conform to others' expectations; she was a 26-year old bride, which was considered quite old in those days.

Walter and Lillie Mae lived on the ranch, raising cattle, pigs, and chickens. Walter, who was educated only through the third grade, became a successful rancher, one who others came to for advice. He belonged to the Cattlemen's Association and was on the Cowley County School Board. He was responsible for putting up bonds and soliciting votes. Because of the community's respect for him, they dedicated the school auditorium in his honor.

Lillie Mae used her nursing abilities to help other women deliver their babies, but she never wanted to be referred to as a midwife. She had worked hard to become a nurse and wanted to be known as one.

After two stillborn babies, Lillie Mae and Walter were thrilled to welcome my mother, who was born at home on April 8, 1917. There was a doctor in attendance, but my mother said there wasn't much for him to do. Walter went to town for the birth certificate and was told that the baby needed a middle name. He came up with the misspelled name of Blanch, and also mistakenly wrote it as her first name, though she was always known as Nadine. Her birthplace was the Township of Windsor, Cowley County, Kansas. Her brother was born 16 months later.

Walter and Lillie Mae remained a little unconventional. In those days, it was highly unusual to have a first child at the age of 35, as Lillie Mae was when my mother was born. They also fostered many children, especially those who lived far from the school. They even let the schoolteacher live with them because her salary was too low for her to maintain her own household.

Walter and Lillie Mae were the eldest children of their respective families. They were the ones who became responsible for family decisions and entertainment when their parents were no longer able. When Lillie Mae's mother invited guests to sit-down dinners, they would hire a maid to cook, but Lillie Mae and my mother were the ones who served the meals. There was no television in those days, so for entertainment they formed circles, sang songs, and square danced. They also played games such as "Skip to My Lou," a game involving couples who choose their partners and stand hand-in-hand in a circle. One boy will have no partner and stands in the center of the circle. He starts by skipping around the inside of the circle and then quickly stealing someone's partner. The new couple then skip around the circle, while the one whose partner was stolen skips after them. If he catches them before they reach the spot he was in with his partner originally, he can take his partner back. If he doesn't catch them in time, he stands in the middle of the circle and starts to skip around until he steals another girl. The person without the partner is the one who chooses which verse everyone will sing on his turn. It was a light-hearted and fun-for-all game that my mother loved to play. She reminisced, "Times back then were difficult, but we knew how to enjoy life."

My mother's first memory was sitting in the back seat of her father's 1917 Model T Ford, holding the clock that had come from England with her grandmother Amos. That was the same clock that had weathered 21 days in primitive living conditions on the lower deck of a ship and was a prized possession. It was large for my mother's small arms, but she held on tightly so it wouldn't shift and break. They were moving closer to town, and she was proud to be the one who had the grave responsibility of holding this clock.

When they got to the ranch, they settled in. On Saturday nights the neighbors came over to play games, dance, and listen to their radio. Knowing they were one of the first families in the county to own a car, they invited the neighbors over for Sunday drives.

My mother proudly recounted that her father told her the barn was a symbol of how well a family was doing. My mother said, "Dad told me that the barn showed that our family was thriving. He said you should always build a barn first, take care of the animals and the animals would then take care of the family." She went on to say, "It was Dad's firm belief that if a man built a nice house with a little barn, he wouldn't do well. Neither would a man do well if he built a large barn and refused to build an adequate house; this would be considered selfish." Her father lived by these rules.

When my mother was six years old, her brother John accidently set the barn on fire. John, afraid of being punished, crawled under the burning barn and refused to come out. Even with his father's pleading he wouldn't come out until his father said he would give him a dollar.

My mother was raised as a Christian in the Methodist church, and the small community shared one church for Presbyterians, Baptists, and Methodists. Methodists believe in the Bible and Jesus Christ as Lord and Savior. One of the beliefs that sets Methodists apart from other Protestants is the belief that people use logic and reason in all matters of faith. They believe that through social service and loving each other they can work for God's love. They believe that Christ died for all people, not just a select few, and they are known for their rich musical tradition where singing is an important part of the service. My mother mentioned to me that the Church of Christ wouldn't participate in the community church because that religion didn't believe there should be musical instruments in the church.

As a Christian she believed God took six days to make the world, and on the seventh day He rested. That seventh day was Sunday. My mother's family and friends revered Sundays because, after the week's heavy daily chores, it was a day of rest and a time for socializing with the people in their church and community. The only time her family didn't go to church on Sunday was one day each year, when a thresher machine containing 12 men came to harvest the grain. My mother's family would serve the men running the thresher a noon meal as their duty to their guests.

Growing up, my mother never felt barriers to playing with children of various other religious or economic backgrounds. The community around them thought her family was different because they had strong English accents, and until their children started school, the children had "terrible" accents as well. My mother's family taught their children that since other people loved and accepted them, they as well should respect differences in other people.

Because my mother lived in a small community, she compared her upbringing to those of her friends. She realized her parents weren't as strict as most. Instead of physical punishment, her parents disciplined her and her brother by taking privileges away. Her parents talked frankly and invited them to help make family decisions. They often gathered for family discussions and openly spoke about their duties and financial responsibilities. She was taught to do right by others, always be herself, and respect her elders.

It was typical in those days for girls to help their mothers with household chores, while boys helped their fathers with outside chores. When my grandmother taught her daughter the routines of the household, my mother strictly followed the example set for her. If my mother didn't do the task well, her mother would patiently do it again. Eventually my mother learned how to do the job right the first time. Her brother learned outdoor chores until he became sickly, so they reversed roles. My mother never mentioned what John's ailments were or how he felt about this role reversal. It was rare to have this kind of gender role reversal in that day and time. He started helping their mother with household duties while my mother helped their father milk the cows, feed the chickens and pigs, and other required tasks. Although it was unusual for a daughter to do a son's chores, my mother thought it was natural. Her mother and father weren't the traditional parents of that time and believed the family should work together as a whole to function.

Even though my mother's parents tried teaching their children right from wrong, it didn't always go smoothly. They were normal mischievous children who sometimes found themselves in trouble for exploring and trying new ideas, even with the best intentions.

Once, their father bought a registered boar to breed, a purebred pig whose name, herd and registration numbers, date of birth, pedigree, and name of owner are recorded with a breed registry association. The children were delighted when the first litter consisted of six piglets. My mother and her brother loved holding and playing with the piglets and started wondering what would happen if they tied their cute curly little tails together. They were too young and naïve to understand the consequences of this experiment. The little piglets started running in circles, squealing and squirming, running into and pulling away from each other. The children stood motionless, unable to stop the frenzy happening before their eyes. It ended when the piglets managed to separate with a final tug, pulling off their respective tails. My mother's father was furious, because now the piglets were unsellable.

As my mother told me this story she smiled, "It was the one time in my life that I knew for sure we were going to get a 'whuppin'."

I don't remember my mother ever mentioning having pets such as cats or dogs, but she did say one of the tailless piglets became a family pet. They named him Freddy. Freddy was a great pet for a while and allowed to come inside or go outside the house at his leisure, until he grew to be over 400 pounds. He grew so big he started becoming destructive. They were unable to stop him from coming inside, and he would burst through the door, causing damage along the way. That was the end for Freddy. In an emotionless voice, my mother casually mentioned that Freddy became dinner.

The only other pet my mother mentioned was Billy, their pet goat. He had the job of pulling the children back and forth to school in a wagon on sunny days. Billy was sold when he started ramming into the side of other people's shiny cars. It simply cost too much money to fix their friends' damaged vehicles. Billy's fate was considerably kinder than Freddy's.

After Billy was sold, my mother and her brother had to find another way to get to school. In that day, it was common for children to ride horses to school if it were too far to walk, and to keep those horses in the barn beside the school until it was time to go home. They brought their own hay to the schoolyard barn to feed the horses throughout the day. My mother and her brother seldom rode a horse because, after Billy, their father usually took them in his Model T Ford. That is, until my mother was able to drive around, at the age of 12.

School lasted from 9:00 in the morning to 4:00 in the afternoon, with an hour for lunch. The teacher made them potato or pea soup or hot sandwiches with a big pot of milk. There were never more than 10 or 12 children in the whole school, and they were taught as a group.

My mother started school when she was eight years old, in a one-room schoolhouse that covered Grades 1 through 5. If her father didn't drive them, he would walk his children to school, and after school they went into town and stayed with their Grandma Amos. The junior high school, which covered Grades 6 through 8, was in town.

When the Great Depression hit in 1929, my mother was in junior high school at the age of 12. She remembered that her father was more fortunate than most because, although he lost his stocks and bonds, he didn't lose his property. Even through the great dust storms he was able to keep his land and help shelter his animals. She remembered the sound of the wind blowing and watching the soil leave one field and go to another. There were no natural grasses or shrubs left for the animals to eat. Families from all around were trying to relocate to anyplace that was safe from the dark cloud of dust that choked and killed animals and pulled small birds from the sky.

Regardless of all that had happened around her in her youth, my mother focused on her good memories. She told me she never felt poor because everybody was poor, and she didn't know any differently. Her aunts were seamstresses, so she was never without clothes. It was a special occasion when her parents let her buy a $5.00 dress from a store for her high school prom. She remembers distinctly that the dress was apricot with a long waist, and layered lace that went down to the middle of her calves.

My mother's family rented an electric freezer in the town of Winfield for a yearly rate of $6.00 to store the beef, pork, and chicken that they raised and slaughtered. Because Winfield was only 18 miles from where they lived, they easily went back and forth to get their meat as needed. There was no refrigeration in their house. She remembered that even though her mother usually made their bread, it cost a nickel a loaf at the store. She also remembered that her father paid $1,200 for a registered bull and 50 head of heifers, to breed them. It always amazed me how my mother could remember the exact cost of purchases. She never lost that ability.

When my mother was a child, her parents took their eggs to town and traded them for coffee, sugar, and other commodities. If they needed more groceries than they were able to trade for, they were allowed to keep a yearly charge account, and pay when the crops came in. They grew several grains on their land and took them to the mill to have them ground into flour. Her father kept one bag for the family and sold or traded the rest.

My mother told me how resourceful her mother was by soaking potatoes overnight, drying them, and using the starch water for their clothes. Her mother also soaked four different grains overnight, and added cream and sugar to make a delicious cereal every morning.

To me, my mother's life sounded idyllic.

CHAPTER 4

Holidays

"Susan? I don't know what to tell ya. I sure wish I could talk to you. Do you know where I am? I sure don't. Can you, can you find out and give me a call? What am I supposed to be doing here? Give me a call, Susan, if you can."

* * *

My mother's family celebrated the holidays at her Grandmother Amos's home. Her family was religious and believed Christmas was Christ's birthday, not everybody else's, so there were no presents or Christmas trees. My mother said she never gave it much thought since that was the way she was raised. Apparently, she changed her mind about Christmas trees and presents by the time she had her own children. When I was young, my family went to the woods and cut down a tree, brought it home, and decorated it. My mother wrapped and put presents under the tree, and on Christmas morning my brother, Jim, and I would wake up early to open them.

Like most children around the world who celebrate Christmas, the season was an exciting one for me. I could hardly wait to open my presents early Christmas morning. We were allowed to open one present on Christmas Eve to calm our excitement a bit, but it didn't really work. I sat and looked at all the other presents, hardly able to contain my excitement. I knew I had to get to sleep so Santa Claus could come and leave a special present and, try as I might, it was difficult to drift off to sleep. My parents always knew when I was sound asleep because I never woke up when they quietly put Santa's present under the tree.

I kept the same tradition for my children. We picked out a small Christmas tree from one of the Christmas tree lots scattered around. I always got someone to help me tie it to the car and took it home so we could decorate it and place lots of presents underneath. I kept the tradition of opening one present on Christmas Eve, and then on Christmas morning the children woke up to a Santa Claus gift of some sort, usually the biggest or most expensive gift they were hoping for.

Even though there were no presents for my mother when she was a child, she said Christmas was an exciting and special occasion. Her family focused more on the gathering of friends and family for an afternoon feast. It represented their feelings of gratitude, happiness, togetherness, and abundance. And always, according to my mother, the Christmas meal deliciously satisfied the soul like no other. There was an abundance of food, such as succulent roasted turkey with bread stuffing, rich brown gravy, creamy mashed potatoes, cranberry sauce, piping hot sweet potatoes, and buttered Brussels sprouts with chestnuts. And it wasn't a holiday meal unless there was a dish of celery, sweet pickles, and black olives, along with bowls of nuts and oranges. For dessert there was always a variety of plum pudding, as well as pumpkin, strawberry rhubarb, cherry, and mincemeat pies. Because there was no refrigeration and nowhere to store food, much of it was left out on the sideboard, covered with a cloth. Even though I realized it was the way my mother was raised, I worried when I saw much of her food sitting on top of the washing machine outside in the garage. This was a practice she had started as a young woman and continued until she could no longer cook meals.

Besides storing our holiday feasts in the garage, my mother also brought other traditions from her family to ours; on most holidays, our family celebrated by first going to church and then gathering for dinner afterward, just as my mother had done since childhood. On Easter, it was tradition, and maybe something of a superstition, to have homemade hot cross buns, which we ate warm from the oven with melted butter on top, a large scrumptious ham, and a big pot of black-eyed peas. Thanksgiving was celebrated with a big feast at the end of the harvest, much like the Christmas dinner, with turkey, dressing, mashed potatoes, sweet potatoes, cranberry sauce, green beans, and finishing with dessert—pumpkin and mincemeat pies. New Year's Day was always celebrated by having pork because pigs rarely walk backward, and the new year represents a time to go forward.

My mother kept some of these traditions alive for her family and I tried to pass some of them down to mine.

CHAPTER 5

Finding Her Path

"Susan? I'm down here in this motel or hotel room and I got your number. So, I don't know what to do because you aren't there. This is Mom. I wish you could give me a call. I'll talk at you later. Bye-bye."

***

After graduating from high school, my mother went to Manhattan, Kansas, to study business at Kansas State College for two years. After college, she started working for different businesses doing accounting and payroll. She was the first to admit that this was unusual for a time when few women worked outside the home. If they did work, it was usually as a secretary, teacher, nurse, telephone operator, retail clerk, or librarian. She liked that she was supporting herself and the feeling of being independent. She lived with other female roommates to help with costs and only went home for the holidays.

My mother met her first husband, John Shaw, at church. As she walked down the aisle to find her seat, her eyes scanned over the heads of several women, and she found herself staring directly into his deep blue eyes. Embarrassed, she quickly turned away, but not before he was able to smile and nod a greeting. She was immediately drawn to this tall, good-looking man, and he looked exceptionally handsome in his military uniform.

Shortly after they started dating, he asked her to marry him. He didn't want to wait, and because she was feeling pressure to get married, she accepted. There was a social stigma for women to be married by the age of 20. She was 20 years old on their wedding day.

They hadn't been married long when John started staying out late drinking. When he returned home, he would often lose his temper and beat her. My mother didn't know if it was because he was an alcoholic, under stress, or simply that she hadn't known him long enough to know his behavior patterns. She wasn't disappointed, however, when he was sent to Germany as an engineer. While stationed there, he met someone else. He wrote and asked my mother for a divorce, only to discover that when a husband was overseas fighting for his country, the law did not allow for a divorce. Because of World War II, my mother stayed married to John for six years. When he came back to the States, they were divorced on the grounds of adultery. Even though it was shameful to get divorced then, my mother's parents were very supportive. Her mother even went to court with her. It was comforting for her to know that her parents were forward-thinking people and didn't worry about what others thought of them. They wanted to see their daughter safe and happy.

My mother had continued to maintain her independence by working and living with female roommates. She found a job balancing books at an accounting firm. Part of her duties were to meet clients from out of town, take them to dinner, and then out dancing. She told me she loved that job and was in no hurry to remarry.

My mother was attracted to men who dressed "spiffy." She especially loved men in uniforms. She met another military man and they started dating. She fell in love after dating him for four months, only to find out he was married. She was brokenhearted but immediately ended the relationship. Even though it was short-lived, my mother kept his picture and gave me pictures of her first husband and this other man to keep when she was in her 90s.

She met my father, James Thomas Williford, while she was working as a secretary to the Sergeant Major of an Army base. My father was a soldier at the time. Because he was gone for extended periods of time traveling for the military, they dated for six years before marrying. It wasn't until he got out of the Army that he proposed to her. They married on September 24, 1947. She was 30 years old. When they married, he had started a business selling cars, but the business went bankrupt and he found himself deep in debt and unemployed. He became depressed, feeling that, as the man of the house, he should be earning enough money to support his wife and future family. My mother could see she needed to do something to save her marriage, and even though she loved working, she came home one day and said, "I quit my job."

"What?" What are we going to do now?" My father was exasperated.

"I don't know. You need to get a job and support us."

The next day he rejoined the Army.

It wasn't long after that my mother became pregnant. She selected her first child's name, which was James Thomas Williford, Jr., born February 8, 1949. My father picked my name, Susan Nadine Williford, born August 21, 1953. He chose my middle name to be the same as my mother's.

CHAPTER 6

Military Life

"Susan? This is Mom. I'm down here at [my phone number]. Would like it if you could give me a call. I do have the right number, I hope. Give me a call if you can. I would like to hear from somebody. I haven't had any calls today. Talk at you later. Bye, bye."

* * *

My mother loved military life. She loved the lifestyle, the parties, and the people they met along the way, and didn't mind moving every three or four years. In 1949, my father was about to be stationed in Germany for four years to help rehabilitate that country after the war. My mother and father stored most of their belongings, left his father Hosey in charge of their bank account, and visited her parents one last time before departing.

It was a warm September afternoon when my father, mother, and brother Jim (who was 7 months old), stopped in Kansas to visit my mother's parents one more time before going overseas. The five of them then decided to visit my mother's brother, John.

My mother's father, Walter, drove, with my father next to him, my mother with Jim in her lap, and her mother in the back seat. They laughed and enjoyed easy-flowing conversations. Walter tried to slow down as he approached a three-way intersection, but when he pumped the brakes, he realized his car was not coming to a stop. My mother held her breath when she noticed a large construction truck heading straight for them. In a desperate attempt, Walter tried to make a sharp right turn to avoid getting hit. My mother remembered the screeching of the truck's brakes and an eerie sound of metal-to-metal crunch upon impact, and then it was over. It did not matter that the one-armed driver of the truck, who was unharmed, was driving an illegally loaded truck with a trailer on the back.

Walter's chest was crushed; he died immediately. My father's head was slashed open, but he didn't sustain serious injury. My mother, who had been breast-feeding Jim, threw her body over his to try and protect him. She suffered whiplash; Jim had a large knot on his head. Neither one was seriously injured. Her mother lay unconscious next to her. An ambulance came and took them to a nearby hospital. My mother, still dazed, found out her mother had suffered a broken femur bone and was injured internally. Her mother died five weeks later in the hospital. My mother found it ironic that her mother died in an accident similarly to the way her mother's own father died. He had been taking the eggs to trade for groceries in town when the horses pulling his buggy somehow became frightened and bolted. He died when he fell off the buggy and broke his neck.

My father had orders to leave for Germany, and the accident didn't change that. My mother and brother stayed behind so she could arrange her parents' joint funerals. Her brother took advantage of her state of mind and talked her into signing over to him, her half of their parents' house and property. After matters were taken care of, she despondently took her child and boarded a plane to meet her husband in Germany.

    She took with her a small picture of a vase with flowers, and a poem she had found tucked away in her mother's purse. My mother commissioned a German artist to recreate the photograph of the vase of flowers in an oil painting. The poem she tucked away in her own purse.

ALONE

I looked out on a peaceful night.
The cold, brown earth was clothed in white
And in the silver stars that told of love
In the pretty blue sky and the air above
I saw my father who was cold and still
Where all was dark and strange and chill.
And I saw my friends of the long ago,
Quietly sleeping under the snow.
Then to my soul from sorrowing long
Came voices singing an old, sweet song,
And from the silence and the pain
Appeared to friends of my soul so plain.
They sat with me in my kitchen old
With no light save the glare from the moonbeam cold.
And I talked with my friends of the long ago
Who are quietly sleeping under the snow.
It seemed that mother was there with me—
It was as plain as plain could be.
A bright light shone on her dear, sweet face,
With a look of joy and peace and grace.
It seemed that Heaven was near that night,

And I forgot the earth all clothed in white
As we talked of the friends of the long ago,
Quietly sleeping under the snow.
Again I walked in the silent night,
The cold, brown earth all clothed in white,
With the silver stars that told of love
In the bright blue sky and the aid above,
And I saw the pines on the wooded hill
And the burial acre stark and still.
And I thought of the friends of the long ago,
Who are quietly sleeping under the snow.

>Mrs. E.D. Cunningham
>Bakersville, Arkansas, January 30, 1921

Once in Germany, my mother found herself surrounded by people who spoke an unfamiliar language. Even at home, where she had thought she would have time alone to grieve, regulations required each Army household to employ a German maid. Surrounded by German-speaking people, my mother learned the language so she would be able to communicate and understand what was being said around her son.

The maid was rough, stubborn, and ill-tempered. My mother immediately disliked her and complained bitterly to my father. And then the maid committed an unforgiveable offense: she placed a freshly baked apple pie on the window ledge to cool in the cold, crisp air. My father, who loved warm apple pie, fired her on the spot. The next maid was accepted and became like a member of the family for their four years in Germany.

On Jim's first birthday, my mother made him a birthday cake from memory. It turned out to be hard as a rock and inedible. She laughed and described how Jim played with that cake for several months until it was so dirty, she finally threw it away.

As Jim approached the age of four, he locked my mother outside on the balcony and wouldn't, or couldn't, let her in. As the story goes, he laughed with glee as she coaxed him, over several hours, to let her in. No luck: she was locked outside until my father came home. Jim claims that's when he learned his first swear words.

That was mildly exciting, but my mother was bored overall. She wanted something to do, and she was, if nothing else, very resourceful. She also had a taste for danger and excitement. Even though she didn't need the money, she sold cigarettes, mayonnaise, and eggs on Germany's black market, for the thrill of it. She kept trading and selling for the four years they lived in Germany, even though her husband, who knew her of her enterprise, could have been court-martialed if she were discovered.

My parents returned to the United States on a sweltering hot August day. From Germany, they traveled by airplane with my four-year-old brother, on their way to a military base in Shirley, Massachusetts, a small town near Boston. It wasn't until they arrived in the States that they discovered that the money they had sent to my grandfather Hosey for the past four years was gone. Instead of depositing it in their bank account as agreed, Hosey had gambled it all away.

My outraged mother also wasn't pleased when she learned that my father had found them a temporary place to stay in a small travel trailer. She was miserably nine months pregnant and could barely fit through the trailer's door, much less move comfortably inside it, especially while dealing with a rambunctious four-year-old. She was relieved when they swiftly moved into military base housing so she could prepare and wait, as comfortably as any pregnant woman in her ninth month could, for my arrival.

PART III

MY STORY

"Uh, Susan?"

"Hi, Mom."

"Where am I? When are you coming to take me home? Who put me here? Who is paying for this?"

"The doctor said you couldn't live alone. The VA is paying for it," I lie.

"You put me here! You get me out of here! I can come live with you."

"I'm sorry, Mom, I work and can't take care of you during the day."

"What happened to my house? Where is all my furniture? Who is paying for all of this?"

"Your house and all your furniture are still there. The VA is paying for this. You don't need to worry about any of this." I lie to her so she won't be stressed. I don't think she needs to know the truth: that she is paying for it out of her savings and the sale of her house.

There is a long pause.

"Dad really did right by me, didn't he, when he set all this up."

"Yes, we are very lucky," I reply.

CHAPTER 7

My Childhood

* * *

The Army military base hospital where I was born had no air conditioning and my mother's labor wasn't easy. After I was born, the nurses placed me in my mother's arms. She started sobbing when she saw my tiny twisted club feet. Unable to console her, the doctor took her into a room where children were missing legs and arms and told her she should feel fortunate that her daughter had something to work with. Fortunately, Massachusetts had an excellent children's hospital. The doctors told my mother that I might never be able to walk, at least not without surgery, and I had to wear steel-soled shoes with a bar attached across the feet at night. Several times a day my mother massaged my feet while I screamed. It was difficult for her to hear my pitiful screams, but she was determined to do everything in her power to enable me to walk.

Ultimately, it was our dog who taught me to walk. When I was two, our boxer dog, Duke, would sit down next to me and let me grab his short stubby tail. Duke would stand up and help me take a few steps before I would fall to the floor. Again, Duke would sit beside me and let me grab his tail. That dog patiently and diligently kept doing this until eventually I learned how to walk without help. When my mother took me to the doctor, he was astonished when he saw me walk.

Duke was a great dog. He understood more than people gave him credit for. Once when my mother had to run into the house, she told Duke not to let me go into the street. She came running back when she heard my screams, only to find Duke sitting on top of me on the sidewalk near the street.

When I was three years old, we moved from Massachusetts to Virginia. We always moved in the hot summer months, and the homes we lived in didn't have air conditioning. My mother put a wet towel over a rotating fan to make a homemade air conditioner. We all gathered around the fan in the living room to cool off. Sometimes we wet washcloths and placed them on our foreheads to help us cool down.

We lived close to the ocean and often went there as a family. We went there one sunny afternoon and I stood staring at the long, sandy beach stretched out before me. Before I knew what was happening, a wave snuck up and I found myself knocked flat on my face. I felt the pull of the current as the wave started receding. I struggled to lift my head out of the water and not get swept back into the ocean. A man saw me struggling and, stooping over me, picked me up as I coughed and sputtered out saltwater. I had had enough of the ocean. As I snorted out saltwater and snot, I somberly went back and sat in the car until my family was ready to go home.

Most of my memories of Virginia are vague, but I do remember my first boyfriend, Donny. We sat together in a field of flowers while he made me flower necklaces and smiled as I put them around my neck. I decided Donny and I would get married when we grew up. One beautiful spring evening when there was the scent of flowers in the air and luscious green lawns stretched before us, I saw my father smoking a cigarette on the porch. Our eyes locked when he noticed me running toward him and I saw a smile spread across his face. When I reached him, I breathlessly sputtered, "Daddy, will you marry us?" as Donny came running up behind me. I thought my father would be delighted and was confused when his expression changed from tender and loving to perplexed and disconcerted. He never answered me.

We left Donny in Virginia and moved to Oklahoma. Oklahoma was where some of my most traumatic experiences unfolded. I turned four years old there. I was upset about the move and didn't understand that moving often was a life I was supposed to get used to. Over time, saying goodbye grew easier, and I stopped bonding with friends so the transition would be more manageable.

We lived in an old two-story home with my bedroom upstairs. My mother had the ability to make every place we lived a warm and comfortable home for us. My bedroom was bright and clean with a double bed, light fluffy bedspread, and yellow curtains.

I was outside playing when a little girl from down the street came up to me and asked if I would like to play with her. She had a cute little black dog with her. We became fast friends as we skipped and hopped and played together with her dog Blackie. Blackie was sweet and good-natured with everybody except the postman.

We were playing one day when the postman came around. Blackie went crazy, running around and snapping at the postman's heels. My friend grabbed Blackie and tried to hold him firmly in her arms. Blackie barked and growled and squirmed, trying to get free. As my friend struggled to contain him, Blackie twisted out of her arms and made a dash for the postman. I heard the sharp barks and then a horrible yelp as the postman grabbed his whip and snapped a quick crack into the air, hitting Blackie in the eye. As Blackie yelped in pain, I screamed and started sobbing uncontrollably. I ran home as fast as I could, in through the kitchen and past my mother, who was sitting at a tiny kitchenette table drinking a cup of coffee. She tried to reach for me, and asked what was wrong, but I ran past her and up the stairs to my bedroom. She didn't follow me or try to console me. I cried until there were no more tears and tried to understand how something so horrific could happen. I couldn't imagine anything worse happening. I was wrong.

I thought my bedroom was my haven until my mother's brother, my Uncle John, came to visit. He was a pilot and decided to fly out to Oklahoma to visit us. He had an infectious laugh like my mother and took an instant liking to me. He teased and played with me, picking me up and swinging me around. I loved the attention.

Late one night, I slowly awoke, aware that someone was standing next to my bed. Hearing my uncle's heavy breathing, I froze and kept very still, sensing something wasn't right. The smell of alcohol on his breath engulfed me as he slid under the covers beside me. I kept my eyes closed tight, pretending I was asleep. I became acutely aware of his large hands as they started to fondle me. I was confused and didn't like what he was doing to me. I was paralyzed with fear. Not knowing what else to do, I continued to pretend I was asleep, desperately hoping he would leave. Instead, his groping became savage and more urgent. At some point, as he continued to ravage my tiny body, I vaguely remember looking down at myself from the ceiling. My brain and body had found a way to protect itself and escape from the trauma. It was a survival technique that helped me endure the ordeal. I don't remember much more, but he must have left during the night, because the next morning when my mother came into my room, he was gone.

She must have known immediately what had happened because she became extremely agitated. As she started jerking the bloody sheets off my bed, I stood quietly in a corner, feeling dirty and ashamed because somehow, I thought, it must surely have been my fault. I must have done something wrong to make him do this to me. My mother moved around the bed as if in a trance. She didn't think to reach down and try to comfort me or tell me it would never happen again. She didn't know she should have taken me into her arms and told me it wasn't my fault. She neither looked at, nor spoke, to me. She was too distraught and angry at her brother.

This was a defining moment in my life. At the age of four, I learned I couldn't depend on anybody to protect me. I became quiet and withdrawn. I was alone. After a trauma like that, it's not unusual to feel shame and guilt. It can take a significant amount of time to get over the memories, the emotions, and the sense of not feeling safe.

Most molesters don't get caught. My uncle never served time but probably molested many children. He lived in a different state and my mother had stopped talking to him, so I didn't hear much about what his life was like. I'm sure my father didn't know about the molestation because he would certainly have beaten or killed him. My mother and I kept it a secret by never telling him, nor did we ever talk about what my Uncle John did to me between ourselves. It was an unspoken truth between us.

I was still quiet and withdrawn when we moved from Oklahoma to El Paso, Texas. It didn't help when we gave Duke to my grandfather Hosey, who lived in the little town of Paducah, Texas, but I knew my grandfather had fallen in love with that dog and would take good care of him. Duke became famous in that town for taking care of children. He saw that they crossed the street safely and kept them safe from any outside danger. His only flaw, if he had one, was that he hated cats and nothing anyone did could train him to leave them alone. Years later I was told they built a statue in his honor.

Before we moved to military base housing, we lived for several months in an old house with a basement. My mother became a den mother for the Boy Scouts, and they convened in that basement. Only boys could join the club, so I wasn't allowed to attend, but she let me serve them refreshments. Taking my time, I carefully carried the tray of lemonade and cookies down the basement steps and enviously watched them for the short time I was allowed to stay.

Still trying to think of ways to console me, my mother took me to the animal shelter and let me pick out a cat. We named him Chester and I loved him dearly. He patiently let me rock him in my tiny rocking chair even though sometimes I rocked over his long tail. Chester was always there for me whenever I needed consoling.

Once, my mother was washing my hair in the kitchen sink when we noticed Chester slink by us. She was using the faucet spray hose to rinse my hair and diverted the hose to spray him. He threw his ears back and tore off at a fierce speed. We both started laughing. I think she was desperately trying to get me to laugh, because I was usually so solemn.

During this time, my mother tried to comfort me by pulling me onto her lap to tell me funny stories. She had a way of telling stories that made us belly laugh until tears came to our eyes. I loved her stories, especially the ones about me, even though they put me in a bad light. I was fond of the story of how I got my middle name all mixed up. My mother was always saying "Susan, no, no!" I was asked my name once when we went to a new Sunday school and I said, "Susan NoNo Williford."

Around this time, I was excited to go to my paternal grandparents' house in Paducah, Texas for Christmas. I didn't know my grandparents well and I was too young to discern the relationship between my mother and my father's parents, but knowing my mother, she never forgave Hosey for gambling away their savings while our family was in Germany.

I remember how tiny my grandmother was, at around 4 feet 9 inches, especially next to my tall, thin grandfather, who was about 6 feet 3 inches. I could smell my grandmother's perfume as she cradled me in her arms and sang, "I love you a bushel and a peck."

While we were visiting them, my grandmother sent me to a store to fetch my grandfather. I don't remember the name of the store, but I called it Parcheesi, like the game. The store owner sent me down to the basement, where I found my grandfather sitting around a table with other men, playing cards. I knew they were gambling.

He looked up with surprise and, putting his right index finger up to his pursed lips, he whispered, "Shh. Don't tell Grandma." I promised I never would.

I loved being reunited with my dog, Duke, and going to the little country store located across the alley from the house. At night, I would either sleep in one of the three screened porches located on the corners of the house, or my grandmother would make me a bed in the living room. I lay at night and listened to the trucks passing by on the highway in front of the house. The sound of the large semi-trucks was comforting as they rumbled down the highway.

My grandparents' house later became a museum called Paducah's 1896 Gober-Baron-Williford House, one of the oldest houses built in that town. I went back to visit once but the house didn't feel the same with mesquite furniture replacing my grandparents' furniture.

Whenever we traveled, we started in the early morning, hours before the birds started chirping or the sun peeked over the horizon. I was asleep when I felt my father's arms wrap around me and softly lift me from my warm bed. He gently placed me on the floor of the back seat of the car, where suitcases, blankets, and pillows made a comfortable bed. I fell back into a blissful sleep as the car started to rumble.

We owned a large car, probably a Chevrolet, that had long, slippery backseats with no seatbelts. When I woke up and sat in the seat, I couldn't keep from rolling from side to side as my father reeled around windy roads. It was hard for me to hang on, and I wasn't heavy enough to stay put.

He got angry with me and yelled, "What's wrong with you, do you have a round butt?" Of course, I did! Didn't everybody?

In those days, there were no air conditioners in cars. We had to roll the windows down to let in the hot breeze. They called it "4 60 AC," meaning four windows rolled down going 60 miles per hour. The heat, pounding down on the car, was unrelenting in those hot, sweltering summer months. Once when my father was in his chewing tobacco stage, he spit out the window and it flew back and hit Jim in the face. Everybody but Jim laughed.

To pass time, my mother turned on the radio. I asked her to wake me up if I was sleeping when my favorite song, "Tom Dooley," started playing. She did as I asked, shouting, "Susan, they're playing 'Tom Dooley!'"

I sat up immediately and started wailing, "Hang down your head Tom [pause] Dooley, hand down your head and cry. Hang down your head Tom [pause] Dooley, poor boy you're bound to die."

Other times, I would ask my father to sing, in his beautiful baritone voice, "The Bulldog on the Bank."

I turned six years old in El Paso. I was finally allowed to buy my first pair of Sunday shoes. I was used to wearing those ugly two-toned Buster Brown shoes that my mother insisted I had to wear because of my feet. Even though I walked normally, my mother always worried that they would revert into the club feet I had been born with. She told me when I was six that she would allow me to have shoes that I could wear only on Sundays. I was excited as we went shopping for my shoes. I didn't find them at the first store, so we went all over town trying on shoes until I found the perfect pair of beautiful black patent leather shoes. I think she was as thrilled as I was to go shopping together.

My beautiful shiny shoes went well with the frilly dresses my mother made me wear. I loved my shoes, but I hated wearing those dresses. When she took me to church one Sunday, I started pulling at the lace on my dress. She tried to stop me, to no avail.

In a stern but deadly-quiet whisper she hissed, "Susan, stop!"

I didn't.

Without a second's hesitation, she firmly grabbed my arm and pulled me to the aisle. I was startled by the firmness of her fingers as she pressed them into my left upper arm. I wasn't really thinking of the consequences as I grabbed one of the large columns in the middle of the church. Clutching the column, I started screaming at the top of my lungs. Embarrassed, she started yanking at me, trying to make me let go. I squeezed my eyes shut and hung on tightly as I continued to scream. As she struggled to make me loosen my grip, she finally managed to wrench me off with a final hard tug. Once out of the church I calmed down. She was red in the face and totally embarrassed. I saw her close her eyes and sigh, and knew I was in trouble.

Once in the car, I kept repeating, "I shouldn't ought to have done that, I shouldn't ought to have done that."

I don't remember what happened when we got home, but I do know that my mother seldom spanked me.

This incident didn't stop us from going back to that church. One Sunday after church, a woman bent down and asked, "Susan? What would you like to be when you grow up?"

I went quiet with thought and then asked, "Can I be anything I want?"

She replied, "Why, yes, of course!"

I responded, "I want to be a bird."

I think I remember this event mostly because of the look of confusion that crossed her face. I mulled the scenario over in my mind for years until I was old enough to understand why she was bewildered by my answer.

It was a hot summer weekend when we moved from the old two-story house to military housing. We put Chester in a pillowcase so he wouldn't freak out in the car. It wasn't a long ride from that neighborhood to the other, but Chester was terrified of car rides. I heard his shrill and pathetic meows, and my heart went out to him. I couldn't stand to hear him in such agony, so I carefully took him out of the pillowcase so I could hold him close to me and comfort him. Chester was a big cat and I quickly realized I wasn't strong enough to contain him in my arms. He began a drawn-out, shrill wailing and howling noise. My mother looked back in time to see him struggling and squirming out of my arms. He flew around in the car wild-eyed as he continued to shriek his dismay. He scampered from the back seat to the front, across my mother's lap, and settled on the top of my father's head, scratching, clawing, and screaming. I was terrified to see the shock, anger, and then calm resignation on my father's face and knew that I was to blame.

My father impatiently bellowed, "Nadine, get this damn cat off my head, I'm trying to drive!"

Eventually, he pulled the car over and we got the situation under control. With Chester firmly contained in the pillowcase, I sat and listened to his panic-stricken snarls feeling helpless that there was nothing I could do. We finally made it to our new home, where I was able to take Chester out of the pillowcase and comfort him.

For some reason, Chester had formed the habit of using my father's shoes as a litter box. Chester disappeared after peeing in my father's shoes one last time. I woke up one morning to find him missing and called out for him, to no avail. I asked my mother to help me find him. I was suspicious of my father because, on an earlier occasion, I had seen him twirl Chester out of the house by his tail after discovering yet again that Chester had peed in his shoes. Both my parents denied that it could have been the cause, but I never saw Chester again. I looked for him every day and grieved his loss. My mother helped me perform a ceremony in his memory, and I had no choice but to accept that he was never coming home.

To help ease the pain of losing Chester, my mother let me have a small lizard. There really is no comparison between a cat and a lizard, but my mother's logic was that the lizard would do nothing to upset my father. I took good care of my lizard and let him crawl over my arms, and he let me gently pet his head. He lived in a beautiful large terrarium, which was decorated with sand, rocks, and cacti. It was beautiful and he could easily laze around or perch on his rock. I went to feed him one morning and found him stiff and nonresponsive and immediately knew he had died. I ran into my room to find a shoebox to bury him in, but upon returning, he was nowhere to be found. Finding my mother in the kitchen, I asked if she had seen him. She turned around to see me holding a box. She turned three shades of red before finally confessing that she had thrown him down the garbage disposal. I couldn't believe she would do that and was quite upset. When my father came home to find me crying, he told me that there would be no more pets. It upset him too much to see me so distraught. I had no choice but to grieve in silence and stayed in my bedroom for the rest of the evening.

I always took refuge in my bedroom, which was my sanctuary wherever we lived. Our home in El Paso, Texas was no exception. I liked living in the military housing, which were single story homes with fenceless yards, built so that the backyards faced each other. It afforded long, wide stretches of grass between the houses and made for a great playing area for children.

One day, my mother looked out the back window and saw a group of boys chasing me down that long stretch of yard. I don't know what I did to make them want to chase me, but I ran as fast as I could, hoping they wouldn't catch up to me. Fortunately, I was a very fast runner. My club feet had long been successfully corrected, and I had no problem running. When I got close to the house, my mother ran out, wildly waving a broom while chasing them and yelling at them to scat. My brother joined her in her efforts to chase them away. If I hadn't been so scared, I would have laughed. Instead, I quickly ran inside the house and watched the commotion from the window.

Looking back, I realize my mother was fiercely protective of her children, and from her stories I gathered it was the way her parents were with her. Despite her protectiveness, she showed little emotion and it was difficult for Jim and me to understand her at times. It was hard to get close to her because she had difficulty expressing emotion, including affection, so we grew up not knowing who she really was.

Even so, I knew my mother was proud of me. She liked the idea that I was a tomboy even though she loved buying me frilly girl clothes. I remember she bought me sleepwear that had a bra and panties with a cute little robe. I was only eight or nine years old, but I decided to wear the bra to school because it made me feel more grown-up. In those days, girls weren't allowed to wear pants to school and our dresses had to be a certain length below our knees, but I found I could wear shorts under my dresses and still do cartwheels and play with the boys. The bra was a little uncomfortable, but I didn't let it stop me from running and playing. When I came home from school, my mother took one look at me and doubled over laughing. I couldn't figure out what was so funny, but she couldn't stop laughing. Going to my bedroom to change clothes, I noticed the bra was wrapped around my neck. My brother Jim saw me and started laughing and poking fun at me. I never wore that bra to school again.

My mother loved to tell the story of when she answered the door one day to a mother and her son. The mother bitterly complained that I had given her son a black eye. My mother summoned me to the door, and when I turned the corner, the woman took one look at me and asked her son in disbelief if that was the little girl who'd beat him up. I was very tiny for my age, and the boy was tall and skinny. As the story goes, she grabbed her son by the ear and left. I have no recollection of this event and wonder if my mother embellished the story a bit and told it so often that it stuck in my memory. What I know is that I was never one to start fights with boys or girls.

Despite my father's no-more-pets rule, we got a chihuahua, choosing that breed because Jim had asthma. That's what I think my mother told my father, anyway, so she could get what he considered a "little rat dog." It was a stretch, but my mother usually got her way, and it worked. We named the dog Pepe, and he slept with Jim every night—until the night Jim passed gas. Jim woke the whole house up, yelling that Pepe had bitten his big toe. Pepe was trapped underneath the covers and was desperately trying to get out. After that, Pepe ended up sleeping on the foot of my bed, and he became my friend—my best friend. He tolerated my dressing him in doll clothes and cuddling with me when I most needed him. He was always there for me.

My mother loved Pepe as well, but more than that she loved playing tricks on my father. When my father traveled, which was often, she would put Pepe's dish of pet food at my father's place on the table. Pepe would jump up on the chair, stand on his back paws, and eat his dinner, and sometimes my mother treated him to a breakfast of cereal and milk. When my father came home from his trips, he never understood why Pepe would sit and growl at him every time he sat down to eat.

I was nine and three-quarters (because when you're nine every month counts) in 1963, when my father learned he'd be stationed in Germany later that year. We were to travel by ship, and dogs were forbidden inside the cabins. Instead, they were placed in cages outside on the ship's deck and forced to endure the cold rain and winds. Owners could visit their pets and let them out of the cages to walk around during daylight hours, but that was all. My father was a man who followed the rules, and he knew that it would be difficult, if not impossible, for such a small dog like Pepe to survive. So we found an elderly woman who was a friend of ours from church to take Pepe. She promised me she would love him and give him steak every night for dinner. I knew she would take good care of him, but I couldn't help but cry when Pepe and I had to part company. Again, my father issued a stern warning: "No more pets."

CHAPTER 8

Pirmasens, Germany

"Uh, Susan? I guess you guys left before I could get my call in to talk back. I'll call back to you in case you didn't get it. But I'm at [my phone number]. Please give me a call and help me get myself straightened out. Would you please?"

***

We were about to go overseas to another country. I felt excited and anxious at the same time, and the knowledge that people would be speaking a foreign language was frightening. I knew we would live on a military base where people spoke English, but three years seemed like a long time to be away from familiarity. I could feel the anxiousness in my parents as well, even though this was their second time living in Germany. I observed the long line of people winding around the ship's terminal as we stood somewhere in the middle, waiting to board.

"Mom, I have to go to the bathroom."

She looked around and found the restroom sign and pointed. "Go quickly and come right back."

I sprinted to the restroom and squirmed as I waited my turn. Before leaving, I was careful to wash and dry my hands. I even took my Alice in Wonderland watch off so it wouldn't get wet. The water felt good and I stood there for a while letting the cool water splash over my hands. When I looked up into the mirror and saw myself staring back, I knew I'd taken too long. I scampered out of the bathroom and searched for my mother. The line hadn't moved much since I left and I saw her looking in my direction, anxious for my return.

It seemed like hours before we finally made it to the boarding dock. The USS *Derby* was a huge and beautiful military ship. It wasn't until we finally set foot on the ship's deck that I looked down at my arm and realized that I had left my Alice in Wonderland watch in the bathroom. I panicked and started to run back and get it, but my mother grabbed me and stopped me from running off.

I cried out, "I left my Alice in Wonderland watch in the bathroom!"

She sternly remarked, "We're boarding the ship now; it's lost."

I pleaded with her; I begged her. It was a birthday present and I treasured it and the little Alice in Wonderland figurine that had come with it. It was the first watch I had ever owned.

My father bent down and asked, "What's wrong?" He could never stand to see me cry.

I sobbed and stammered, "I left my Alice in Wonderland watch in the bathroom!"

Grabbing my mother by the arm, he said, "Nadine, I'll be right back."

She reached out to grab hold of him, but he scurried off before she could reach him.

Surely, the ship couldn't leave without him. I was worried he wouldn't get back in time to board. We were on deck, holding on to the railing and looking in the direction my father had gone. I felt a surge of panic grip me as the loud horns started blasting. I stared at the spot where he had disappeared from my sight. Eventually, I thought I spotted him running toward us, and then recognized him as he drew nearer. He looked up and saw me holding on to the railing. A smile spread across his face as he held up my watch so I could see it. He jumped on board just as they were removing the gangway from the ship. Somehow, he had managed to find and return to me my prized possession.

It took seven days to sail to Germany. Our compact quarters featured two bunkbeds lined on each side of the room and one little porthole window located high above our heads. Jim and I endured on one side of the room and my parents on the other. Jim claimed the top bunk leaving me to settle in the bottom bunk.

I was excited as we walked along the narrow passageways to the dining hall, submitting to the gentle rolling of the huge ship. We saw many families heading in the same direction. There was one family who had six children, who lined up from youngest to eldest holding hands so nobody would get lost in the crowd. I was impressed with how well-behaved even the youngest children were.

When we found our table, we sat down to order dinner.

I saw what I wanted on the menu and said, "Mom, I want the rabbit."

My mother stared at the menu before she realized what I was ordering.

"Susan, that's not rabbit, it's Welsh rarebit. It's an English muffin with melted cheese on top of it."

"No, Mom, that's rabbit. That's what I want," I insisted.

She let me order it knowing that if I didn't like it, she would. She ordered the chicken, knowing what I like. When the meal was served, I sat in disappointment staring down at my food but saying nothing. Quietly, my mother sighed while reaching over and trading our plates. The rest of the journey on the ship was uneventful and after seven days at sea we docked in a German port.

For three years we lived in the small town of Pirmasens, Germany, where there was an Army base, but my father worked about 30 miles away in Landstuhl. When we arrived, there was a two-month waiting list for housing on the military base. We ended up living on the third floor of a German home. The first floor was occupied by another American family and the second floor was where the German family lived. Our kitchen was in the room with the steep slope of the attic, and my father constantly hit his head when he stood up, shouting obscenities every time. The combination bathtub/kitchen sink and only heater in the apartment were in that kitchen. My mother jubilantly commented that by doubling the bathtub for a kitchen sink, she never had dry skin.

I often got up early on cold crisp mornings to go to the bathroom. To get there, we had to leave our warm apartment and head down a flight of stairs; it was located on the left side of a narrow hallway. I immediately awakened from a stupor when I sat on the cold toilet seat and was dismayed to discover that the toilet paper felt like sandpaper. The door into the apartment automatically locked and couldn't be opened from the outside. I would hear the door lock click behind me, reminding me that I wouldn't be able to get back into the apartment.

Once, as I sat shivering in my thin nightgown, my father opened the door to leave for work.

"Susan, what are you doing out here?"

I whimpered, "I had to go to the bathroom and forgot that the door locks behind me."

"Why didn't you knock and wake us up? I would have come and let you in," he said in an irritated tone.

"I don't know. I didn't want to disturb anybody."

I repeatedly did this, morning after morning, for the two months we lived there. Each time, my father opened the door to find me sitting on the step waiting to get back in. It never occurred to me to put something in between the door and doorjamb to keep it from locking behind me.

The American family on the first floor had two young boys whom I sometimes tried to play with. They saw me sliding down the banisters one morning and started doing the same. I intuitively knew when the landlady was looking and made sure she never caught me. She got furious with the boys and told them they should learn manners from me. I secretly smiled as they squealed that I also was sliding down the bannisters, but she didn't believe them. I never told her otherwise.

It felt strange walking down the streets of the German town, not understanding what people were saying. I would go into a store only to realize I was unable to read the words on labels. Sometimes I could figure out what was inside the canned goods by recognizing the pictures on the outside of the cans.

I met a little German girl and tried to play dolls with her. She said something in German, and I tried communicating in English. We finally gave up. I entertained myself by strolling around the streets and felt lost when I couldn't understand conversations or make sense of the street signs. I was confused and lonely and missed my home country terribly.

My mother made the most of it. Not by playing the black market like she did the first time they were in Germany, but by making dishes like homemade applesauce with currants, and turning sour milk into cottage cheese.

My father had to take the car to work with him, so our family went to the commissary to shop for groceries on the weekends. Once when my parents and brother went out, they left me in charge of answering the door for two American soldiers who were expected to come to the apartment for a meeting with my father. I felt very grown up, having this responsibility and getting to stay in the apartment by myself. When they knocked on the door, I invited them to come inside and wait. I had been in the bathroom experimenting with my hair. I wasn't very skilled at putting my hair up and I'm sure it was a mess. With a glint in their eyes and a playful smile they praised me about how grown up I was and how pretty my hair looked.

The evenings were my favorite part of the day because my family gathered around the kitchen table playing the card game pinochle. We played with two decks and after I arranged my hand, one of my parents would fan out my cards for me because my hands were too small to do it myself. Pinochle is a complicated game played with a deck of 80 cards made up of only aces, tens, kings, queens, and jacks, where you need to communicate with your partner and learn how to bid. We had started playing canasta when I was about six and then graduated to pinochle when I was nine. By then, I'd learned how to count cards and read my partner's playing techniques. Most of the time I enjoyed playing, but sometimes I felt it was too much pressure. My father was almost always my partner and Jim my mother's. There was a slight reprieve in the games when my father bought a large bottle of German Parkbrau beer, which I loved.

"Pass the beer around the table, please" I asked, making my voice small so my father wouldn't notice how much of it I was drinking.

Once, I must have started acting a little tipsy because my father suddenly pointed his finger at me and blurted out, "Looky there! She's getting drunk! That's enough beer for you, Susan!"

After about a month, we were excited to move onto military base housing. That meant that we would live and go to school among other American families. The first apartment we stayed in was on the fifth floor and had eight bedrooms. These apartments were usually reserved for large families, so it was once again only temporary housing for us. Jim and I entertained ourselves by sliding down the long hallway in our socks. The apartments had no elevators, so we got plenty of exercise climbing up and down the stairs. In the basement, each apartment had a storage room where we could set up a playroom. There was also a large room with several old wringer washing machines. My father helped my mother carry the dirty clothes down to the basement, helped her wash them, and then carried the wet clothes back up the stairs so she could hang them to dry in the apartment.

It was while we were living in this apartment that my parents' good friends Reese and Marvin moved to Germany, close to where we were living. Marvin was also in the military and had become good friends with my father. We first met them in El Paso, Texas, and I remember visiting them because they had a medium-sized poodle named Charlie. Reese warned me that Charlie didn't like children; she was concerned that he might nip at me, but instead, Charlie and I immediately bonded. When Reese noticed how Charlie took to me, she decided to get to know me better. I was ecstatic to see my friend Charlie in Germany. I asked Reese how Charlie managed on the ship since we couldn't bring Pepe. She leaned down and whispered that she visited Charlie every day and when nobody was looking, she snuck him inside their cabin at night. She was unable to have children of her own and Charlie was her child. Reese sympathized with me, knowing how much I missed Pepe.

Much to my father's dismay, Reese showed up at our apartment one day holding a little black puppy. I mistakenly thought cheetahs were the big black cats, so I named our puppy Cheetah. Unfortunately, the puppy was already quite sick, and died while my parents were in the basement washing clothes. I ran down the flights of stairs as fast as I could to get my parents, but there was nothing they could do. My father again declared, "No more pets!"

After living in the eight-bedroom apartment for a while, we moved to a smaller apartment located on the second floor. It was easier for my mother to go to the basement to wash clothes. She allowed us to play in the basement storage room assigned to us.

One day, I found a small pack of stale cigarettes in a box of C-rations and with another friend, we decided to try smoking. The storage room had a window at the very top of the room looking out into the street. We opened the window so the smoke would go outside. There was a knock on the door and my mother asked what we were up to. Of all the many times we played in that room, how did she know this one time we were smoking? I opened the door and looked up at her.

She nodded and said, "If you are going to smoke, I want you to smoke in front of me."

I hated it and never smoked again.

Every summer I stayed with Reese and Marvin for a couple of weeks in the country. They lived on the second floor of a house they shared with a German family, who lived on the first floor. The German family had a daughter, Elizabeth, about my age, who could speak English. We became friends, and she came upstairs to sleep with me when I went to visit. My parents and Reese and Marvin often visited back and forth. Sometimes I came home from school to find Charlie waiting for me by the door. He was so excited to see me that he jumped up and put his paws around my waist so we could dance around the apartment.

Reese and my mother became fast friends. They had similar mischievous ways and created all kinds of havoc. They made a "G.I. punch," which I wasn't allowed to drink, but I was invited to play charades with them. I think the adults gave me phrases or names of movies that I could easily act out. I loved being included in their games.

Reese liked how adventurous I was, especially when it came to food. I loved just about anything she cooked, including bear, venison, rabbit, and even cow's tongue; however, I never took a liking to cow liver or brains. She tried to show me how to make a cake once, until I lifted the spinning beaters from the mixer and cake batter splattered all over the kitchen. She couldn't believe what I had done and asked me why I did it. I shrugged my shoulders and replied, "I don't know."

Once, the German family gave me a pet rabbit, which I could play with when I visited. I named her Suzie and played with her whenever we visited. At dinner one evening, Reese made the comment, "Well, here's to Suzie!"

Evidently, Suzie was really a Sammy, and they ate the males. I looked over at my mother in time to see her close her eyes and sigh as though she were silently saying, *Why would you say that, Reese!*

I was appalled and sick to my stomach. I couldn't eat my rabbit.

During one of my stays with Reese, Charlie got caught up in the lawn mower. Reese ran out shrieking for me to run quickly to the back gate of the military base down the street and get Marvin. I ran as fast as I could, but the guards stopped me at the gate. I gasped for breath and tried to tell them I needed to get Marvin because our dog was badly injured. It must have been obvious that even though I was a young girl, I was an American. One of the guards smiled, pointed me to a building, and with a glint in his eyes told me I would find Marvin in there. I ran inside, stopping briefly to adjust my eyes to the dark. I spotted Marvin sitting at a bar having a drink. I was young, but I knew then that Marvin had a drinking problem. His eyes lit up when he saw me and he tried to introduce me as his daughter, but I was in no mood for small talk. In that moment, I noticed a sadness in his eyes and knew he wished he could have had a daughter of his own. I told him the situation and we left to get the car so we could drive Charlie to a vet. Charlie needed stiches in his neck but was otherwise fine.

Marvin didn't like to travel, so Reese came with us when we went on vacations. Reese wasn't a small woman, and the five of us shared a room; we managed, even though it was somewhat cramped. I gave her back rubs—she complimented me on how strong my tiny hands were—and we talked for hours.

My mother and she had a similar, contagious way of laughing. I loved overhearing their mischievous adventures. When we went out to eat, we shared our food so we could sample the many varieties of food served. Reese quietly stole the ceramic salt cellars with the little spoons. She had such a big purse she could also steal beer mugs and the like. She winked at me and I accepted her habit and kept quiet.

At one restaurant we visited in France, there was a large fish tank, to choose your own fish to eat. When they brought it out on a plate, I squeamishly looked at it, with its one eye staring up at me, and couldn't bring myself to eat it. Reese took the head off and tried to show me how to eat the eyes, but I couldn't watch, not wanting any part of it.

Back on the military base, my father formed a carpool to take turns driving the long, treacherous route to work each day. The winding mountainous roads had no guard rails, and when it was foggy or icy, or both, it was a nerve-wracking drive. His days were long and stressful and most days he came home late and drunk.

I overheard my mother say to him one night, "Oh, Willie, not again! This is happening almost every night now. If you keep this up, I'm filing for divorce as soon as we get back to the United States."

Even though I didn't understand exactly what was going on, I felt the tension and had trouble sleeping at night. I lay in bed and kicked as hard as I could to keep from feeling the pain in my stomach. My mother often heard me and lay down beside me until I fell asleep.

My father wasn't a healthy man throughout most of his life and developed congestive heart failure, blocked arteries, and emphysema. He had his first heart attack at 48, when I was 10 years old. He was a sergeant in the Army at this time and was taken to the Landstuhl military hospital. When we went to see him in the hospital, I was frightened and shocked to see all the tubes and big machines he was hooked up to.

My mother noticed how overwhelmed I was, so she bent down close to me and in a soft casual voice said, "Don't push that button honey, you'll blow your daddy up."

His eyes flew open. He looked around wildly and then settled his gaze on me. He looked at me suspiciously, but I understood my mother was trying to distract me from the impact of the situation. It was her dark sense of humor. After he recovered from his heart attack, he was transferred to Pirmasens, where we lived, and their relationship got better. He stopped staying out late and drinking every night.

Even though the sick feeling in my stomach never completely went away, I have good memories of our time in Germany. Halloween was always fun. All the children dressed up in costumes and ran up and down the stairwells, asking for candy. So many children came to our door, that my mother ran out of candy. She resolved the problem by putting a nylon stocking over her head and going trick or treating herself. She looked hilarious but fit in because she was a small woman. Only one person asked her if she wasn't a bit old for trick or treating.

The summer months were usually cold and damp and there were seldom more than three consecutive days of sunshine. The terrain was a luscious green, though in the winter, the fog was so thick at times that I couldn't see the end of my fingers from my outstretched 10-year-old arms. I walked to school, and it was challenging to find my way on those days. Standing outside my apartment building, I blindly headed with outstretched arms toward the building across the street. Thankfully, the buildings were large and wide with three stairwells to a building. I usually ran into a building I recognized by heading down to the basement where we often played. From there, I steadily felt my way along until I reached the end of the building. Taking a deep breath, I gathered up my courage and stepped out into the open, walking at an angle, and hoping to find the blacktop path that would lead me to school. If I got lost along the way, I would try to backtrack, but with no visibility I easily got turned around. I knew that the fog would lift at some point and I would be able to see better, even if that meant I missed the morning classes, but that never happened.

Once, while walking home from school, I felt a strong hammer-like bolt hit me on the top of my head. I looked up to see lightning a second before I heard the loud clap of thunder. I was not aware that my mother had been looking out the window. As I came running into the safe haven of our apartment, my mother was laughing. She said she saw me jump three feet straight up in the air and start running as fast as I could to get home. I was still too terrified to laugh with her. Obviously, the lightning was far enough away that it hadn't actually hit me.

At school, I discovered that I was the second fastest runner. Boys lined up with me only to find themselves left behind when I started running. There was only one boy who was faster than me, an African American boy named Marty. We became good friends.

He came to the door of our apartment once, to ask if he could borrow my spelling book. He stood at the door while I ran to get the book and upon returning, he smiled and said he would return it the next day at school. My father saw the transaction and asked to speak with me. At the end of his two-hour lecture, he asked me if I understood him. I hadn't understood at all, but I nodded in agreement anyway to avoid more lecturing. He had used the word "passion" several times, so I looked it up in the dictionary. I still didn't understand and mulled that memory over in my mind for years before realizing that even though my parents had raised my brother and me to not be prejudiced, my father was worried that I would grow up and marry an African American.

At this time, I was still quiet and shy, so my teachers and my mother thought it a great idea to sign me up for the talent show competition at my school. I didn't want to participate because I thought it would be humiliating, and I agonized over how to get myself out of it. My mother suggested I play "The Old Rugged Cross" on my recorder. Did she honestly think that was a good idea, or did she know that was the only song I knew how to play? I tried everything I knew to not participate but the teachers insisted and pushed me onto the stage. I stood there with the recorder in my hands looking around: it was either do nothing, or play. I looked down from the stage and saw my classmates gazing at me with interest, then with empathy, as I put the recorder to my lips and belted out the simple tune. I was thankful that nobody laughed out loud. I competed with many contestants who were much more talented, and I didn't win the competition.

Even though I was extremely quiet and shy, acting didn't frighten me. I was asked to play the role of a bride in a Raggedy Ann doll play. I memorized my lines, and my mother made my stage costume, a wedding gown. When I went onstage, I heard the girls in the audience sigh. The boy playing the groom was tall and thin, while I was tiny by his side. We looked like the couple placed on a wedding cake. I was a bit nervous at first but found that acting was something I was good at. I was comfortable pretending to be someone else.

After I turned 11 years old, my mother went to the hospital for a few days for an uncomplicated operation. My father decided I was old enough to make us dinner. I took on the challenge and spread peanut butter topped with marshmallow whip on slices of bread.

I then placed them in the toaster oven and let the marshmallows come to a beautiful brown color and gooey concoction. I thought I'd made one of the best dinners ever. My father said nothing as he ate with a sheepish grin on his face. The next night, he made us bacon and eggs.

Around this time, I started developing breasts. I was such a tomboy that I didn't want to be bothered with wearing a bra. I was barely developed, but enough that I could no longer wear tight-fitting shirts. The boys my age started playing a game of snapping girls' bras. One boy came over to me, reached behind my back, but couldn't find a bra to snap. He yelled "oops!" before moving on. I was so embarrassed. I went home and told my mother what had happened. In those days, there were no training bras or anything small enough to fit me, so my mother bought a very pretty bra, put her seamstress skills to work, and cut it down to size. I wore it every day from then on.

After three years in Germany, my father came home and asked if we wanted to stay one more year in Germany or if we wanted to go back to the United States. My mother, brother, and I unanimously wanted to return to the States. My father would have been promoted if he had stayed, but agreed with the family decision to return.

There was a poem about Pirmasens that my mother retyped on her cursive typewriter. The author is unknown.

PIRMASENS

Across the hills and valleys,
Pirmasens is the spot.
We are doomed to spend our time,
In the land that time forgot.
Down with beer and cognac,
We're gallant dependent true.
Right in the middle of nowhere,

Nine million miles from you.
Dropouts of Pirmasens,
They earn their measly pay.
Working in the commissary,
At two and a half a day.
In our sacks we dream at night,
Of our lovely stateside Miss.
To hold her in our arms again,
And steal a treasured kiss.
Then in heat and cold we march,
To catch our antique bus.
Oh what a miserable day we have,
When our teachers get hold of us.
No one knows if we're alive,
No one gives a damn.
The old gang has forgotten us,
We're owned by Uncle Sam.
This time we spend in Pirmasens,
Is time we'll never miss.
Just don't let the draft get you boy,
And for God's sake don't enlist.
But when the Pearly Gates,
Come in the dependents view.
Our frowns will turn to laughter,
And the joke will be on you.
For once in sight of heaven,
You will hear St. Peter yell.
Come spend your time in heaven,
You've spent your time in hell!!

We sailed back to the United States on a military ship, where there were activities such as ping pong and swimming. You could also lounge around and read a book or play cards. In the evening, the adults could dance or play bingo. Because I was turning 12, I got to play bingo with the adults at night. I felt very grown up and was delighted when I won 10 dollars.

One day, I was on the top deck of the ship when a strong gust of wind almost knocked me off the deck and into the ocean below. I struggled, grabbing onto anything solid, crawling along the deck until I was back inside. I saw the crew stringing ropes down the hallway, for passengers to hang on to. We were told we were going through a hurricane and if it got too dangerous, we might have to turn back. The waters were rough, crashing over the high decks and causing the huge ship to rock.

One woman, who was very afraid, asked how much further we had to go.

Her husband said, "We're only three miles from land."

She looked surprised. "Really?"

"Yes," he said, "straight down."

Mortified, she started crying. I felt sorry for her but was not afraid. Maybe I was too young to realize the danger we faced. I found it all very exciting and was fascinated as I listened to the angry sea raging and howling, rocking the ship, and throwing its furious white talons against the porthole windows.

Everybody around us became sick. We were one of the few families who avoided seasickness because my mother brought apples and crackers back to our room and made us eat often. When we went to the dining hall, I saw very few people sitting at the tables, and I wondered why they served soup. Even though there were guards to keep the bowls from sliding off the tables, the soup sloshed over the sides of the bowls as the ship rocked.

Although seven days on the ship seemed like an eternity, the morning I woke to see the Statue of Liberty, I started to panic. I was excited, yet nervous, about going back to America. I wondered, *Am I ready for this? Will I fit in?*

I stood in awe as I looked out over the city of New York. I had a feeling of pride in being an American that tugged at my heart. Even though Germany is beautiful, there is nothing like the United States of America. It is home. It is where I belong. When we got off the ship and stood on solid earth, we had wobbly sea legs. I fell to my knees and kissed the ground. The sick feeling in my stomach that I had the whole time we lived in Germany was gone.

We watched as they transported the cars off the ship using a crane. To our astonishment, we witnessed the crane drop our car. When we were able to get inside and drive off, the car still ran, but every time we hit a bump, the windows fell straight down. We headed off across the country toward the stark deserts of El Paso, Texas.

CHAPTER 9

El Paso, Texas

"Susan? This is Mom and I wish you would give me a call so you can straighten me out. I'll talk at you later. Bye-bye."

* * *

The trip across country was long and arduous. I slept, or watched the various terrain pass by. My mother brought a pot for me to pee in so my father didn't have to stop so frequently. If he did stop the car, it was on the side of the road; we opened both front and back doors and squatted in the middle, not really caring if anyone in the cars driving by saw us. After an especially long day of traveling, we rented a room at a roadside motel with two beds.

After eating dinner at a small diner, we settled in for the night. Jim slept with my father and I slept with my mother. Evidently, my mother had the worst of it, as I kicked and hit her in my sleep. My mother told me of the time my father and she rented a motel room.

The motel beds in those days often had vibrating mattresses. You put in a quarter and it vibrated for about an hour. My father loved those vibrating beds; my mother detested them. He put in a quarter while she gritted her teeth and waited, without complaint, for the motion to stop. That was so typical of my mother, to stay silent in her passive-aggressive manner while expecting my father to know what she did and didn't like. When the mattress finally stopped, she sighed to herself in relief and slowly started drifting off to sleep. My father reached over and put in another quarter.

My mother stopped cuddling, kissing, and hugging me about the time I turned 12. She stopped displaying much emotion or affection, period, probably because it was the way she was raised. At some point in my adult years, I began to realize that I had stopped hugging my own children. I reflected on my life and remembered how I was raised. I wanted to stop this pattern from being passed down to future generations and resolutely kept hugging my children until I felt comfortable with it. My mother saw me hugging them as they grew older, and in turn, she kept hugging them as well. The first time she hugged me, I was in my early 30s. It took me by surprise, and I was uncomfortable at first, but eventually we worked through it, and hugging became a natural part of our lives.

Instead of showing emotion, my mother liked to tease, but her incessant teasing made me feel inadequate. There was no right way to react. If I got angry, she laughed and made fun of me. If I cried, she teased me. If I showed no emotion, she teased me for pouting. I finally got to the point in my life when I stopped letting it bother me, but it took many years to get there.

All the same, I inherently knew she deeply loved me and, on an even deeper level, needed me. I was very young when she started expecting much more from me than a child should have to bear. She leaned on me for strength. She never wanted the responsibility of making decisions about anything. What she wanted was for someone else to make the decisions, so she could complain about them.

First, it was my father who made the decisions for her. He found the houses for them to live in, picked the cars they bought over the years, and usually made even the most minute decisions—unless I was around to help make the decisions for them. He took in stride her retributions, knowing he would always be blamed for any failure. After he died, I shouldered the full responsibility for the decision-making.

When we got to El Paso, I started eighth grade. My mother always had access to a car, but she had never given me a ride to school and wasn't about to start then. Not in the thick fog, not when the snow came up to my waist in Germany, and not even when there were sandstorms in El Paso. I hated the sandstorms. It was impossible to see. You couldn't keep your eyes open or they would get blasted with sand. During one of those storms, I was stuck at the school entrance. All the other children's parents had already picked them up, and I was the last one waiting for a car ride that I knew would never come. One of my teachers saw me standing there, took pity on me, and offered me a ride home. I was a little embarrassed but too grateful for her kindness to pass on her offer. She threw her sweater over me and we made our way to her car. When she dropped me off, I found my mother sitting in an overstuffed chair reading. She looked up as I bustled into the house.

"My teacher had to give me a ride home because you weren't there to pick me up. All the other kids' parents came to the school to pick them up," I complained.

I waited for a response or reaction of some kind, but my mother remained silent and motionless, revealing no remorse. I walked over to the window and looked out, watching the swirling sand, and feeling thankful to be safely home.

Other than the weather, I liked living in El Paso. This was a stage in my life that took me through many physical, mental, emotional, and social changes.

Five girls who had been friends for years pulled me into their circle. We called ourselves "The Sexy Six." I was at an age where I noticed boys, but I was too afraid to start a conversation or show any interest. One time, my mother answered the door to find three boys who asked if I could come outside and talk to them. I knew one of them was interested in me, so I ran to my room and refused to go outside. She looked concerned when I didn't want to go and talk to them, but said nothing and told them I wasn't available to come outside at that time.

One might think that a child of the military would be outgoing and friendly, but I was still incredibly shy, and rarely spoke up. No matter how often I told myself with each move that I was going to change, I never could. It was a teacher who noticed that I was a very fast runner and helped me sign up for track. I won first- and second-place ribbons at the girls' state track meets. My mother seemed proud and came to the meets to watch me run. There was one relay race where we joined the boys. As I intensely studied my teammate so I would recognize him when I passed the baton, he glanced over at me. I realized with horror that it was the same boy who had come to my house to talk. I wanted to crawl into a hole, but there was no place to go. He must have noticed how embarrassed I was, but he said nothing. I was still one of the fastest runners in my school, boy or girl, so I did well.

When I was 12 years old, my mother got sick with the flu.

My father, looking tired and worn down, said, "Susan, your mom is very sick. I would like you to help out by washing the clothes. Can you do that?"

"Yes, I can do that," I said.

I started by sorting the light- from dark-colored clothes and filling the bathtub with water to wash my mother's delicate lingerie, which I had seen her do many times. My father came into the bathroom and saw the bathtub filled with clothes.

"What the hell are you doing, washing all the clothes by hand?"

"No Dad, this is how Mom does it ...," but before I could finish, he lost complete control of his temper, raised up his hand, and started slapping me.

I'd already put a load in the washing machine, but he hadn't noticed.

"Please! I *am* washing the clothes!"

He didn't hear me as he continued to yell and slap me.

"*Please, stop Dad*," I sobbed, as he continued to slap me hard across the face.

"*Please Dad, stop*!" I sobbed trying to get the words out in between the slaps.

After he was spent from slapping me, he pointed a finger at the heaping clothes and spat, "You will finish washing these clothes the right way and hang them outside to dry!" Red-faced and still steaming, he finally left me to finish the chore.

My face stung while I finished washing the clothes and headed outside to hang them. The bright sun pained my swollen eyes, and I could hardly keep them open as I hung the clothes on the clothesline.

My mother sat and said nothing while all of this was going on. Afterward, I went to my bedroom and stayed there the rest of the night. I told myself I would get sick or die and that would teach them! Much later that evening, I overheard my mother.

"Willie, Susan was washing the clothes they way I always do. She had my lingerie in the bathtub, not the clothes that go in the washing machine. Susan did nothing wrong," she explained.

I could not see their faces and heard nothing else. My father never came to my room to see how I was doing, or to apologize to me. Many years later, I sometimes pondered my mother's behavior. Why didn't she try to stop him?

The closest I came to answering that question was that what she really wanted was for me to be an extension of herself: an uncomplaining, though passive-aggressive, woman who silently dealt with everything that came her way. I tried to walk a path somewhere between what I wanted and what she wanted so we both could be happy. I resisted getting to know my mother. I didn't want to lose myself in her.

Because my mother expected more of me than I could possibly give her, I became emotionally distant from her. She craved visits, lunches together, or shopping, but instead of appreciating the time we spent together, she tried to manipulate me, or demand more. Nothing I did was enough; she always wanted more. I couldn't satisfy her need for control. It was with sheer determination that I managed to live my life for me and spend time with her when I could, without feeling guilty.

CHAPTER 10

Susanville, California

"Susan? If I'm getting you, give me a call at [my phone number]. Would like it if you would give me a call if you can. I would like to hear from somebody. I haven't had any calls today. Talk at you later. Bye-bye."

* * *

From Texas, we moved to Susanville, California, a little town in Northern California about an hour and a half north of Reno, Nevada. Before moving there, Jim and I had no idea where Susanville was, but were excited about the move to California. We envisioned swimming in the ocean, walking on the beach, and watching the surfers, maybe even learning to surf ourselves. You might imagine how surprised we were when we arrived. Susanville is a long way from any beaches, and there had been an unexpected snowstorm in July! We looked at each other with disappointment in our eyes.

In reality, Susanville was a quiet little town nestled up against a mountain of pine trees with an elevation of about 4,000 feet. In 1967 there were about 7,000 people with one main street and no stoplights. There was one high school, which is where I went, and one junior college, which was where Jim went. I began calling it a "soap opera town" because everyone was into each other's business. The townspeople loved nothing more than to spread good, juicy gossip.

After retiring from the Army, my father got a job at the Sierra Army Depot at Herlong, California, about 45 minutes from Susanville. Built in 1942 to store ammunition safely away from a feared Japanese attack on the coast, the Sierra Army Depot was also used for storage of unarmed nuclear weapons. Herlong was a good location for a facility storing nuclear weapons because it was a dry, isolated area. I remember a time when my father came home from work early because someone had made a mistake; they shut the whole building down and sent everybody home. I think he said something about Susanville almost being removed from the map. He also told me once that he had to dip his hands into some type of dangerous liquid while working at Herlong. He never talked much about what he did while in the military, but I know it had something to do with missiles and nuclear weapons.

Reese and Marvin had also bought some land just outside Susanville and were waiting for us to arrive. Marvin was already working at Herlong and was excited when my father took a position there. Reese and my mother picked up where they left off, creating mischief and having fun. My mother loved to recapitulate the story of when Reese bought a horse and tried to get it into the horse trailer. My mother stood back, watching and laughing, until she realized Reese didn't know what she was doing and couldn't get the horse to obey her commands. Because my mother had been raised on a ranch with horses, she knew what to do, and finally went over to help.

Susanville was also where Reese taught me how to make a delicious spaghetti sauce, broil steak, and make her famous Rancho Enchiladas. Years later, Reese and Marvin moved to Missouri, bought some acreage, and raised horses. My mother stayed connected by writing letters and sending Christmas cards.

I saw Reese one more time around 1982, when I was in my late 20s. She came out to visit my parents and wanted to see me again. I was a single mother, and she reminded me, as my mother often did, that it was better to marry a rich man than a poor one. Marvin had divorced Reese and married another woman, which was a contentious subject for Reese. My mother was loyal to Reese, but she understood why the marriage failed: Reese constantly criticized Marvin and told him how stupid he was. They fought constantly. After they returned home from a road trip, Marvin got out of the car and told Reese he was through. He continued to help Reese and had to put her in a home when she started losing her mind. Reese died of Alzheimer's disease.

The move to Susanville took place the summer before I started high school. The town was small, and I found it hard to make friends. Jim was starting his first year in college, so we did not hang out together or share the same friends. Because I was so shy and quiet, the girls thought I was a snob. It didn't help that the boys flirted with me, making their girlfriends jealous. I kept to myself, walking to and from school alone. Weekends seemed endless and were almost unbearable. I was lonely but endured and found solace in books.

At school, there was a boy who stood in a corner and watched me walk to my classes each day. I learned his name was Barry. He was a popular senior, and I was a freshman. Though I tried to ignore him, he spotted me in the halls and flirted with me every chance he got. He stepped in front of me one day and wouldn't let me pass. His brown eyes were twinkling as he stood there, smiling down at me.

We silently stood face to face for a while until I started to feel uncomfortable. When he finally spoke, he asked if I would go to a dance with him; I accepted.

Barry and I became inseparable. We slowly got to know each other and I, at the young, tender age of 14, fell in love for the first time, believing there could be no one else in my life. I was accepted as Barry's girlfriend and started making friends; in fact, I immediately became popular in my school. Barry had a car, so he chauffeured me and my girlfriends around town. For the first time in a long time, I started feeling content with life. I was also young, naïve, and trusting, not able to see or understand the red flags that began to pop up in our relationship.

Once when Barry and I got into a huge fight, he decided to take me home. I didn't like his controlling behavior and in as stern a voice as I could muster, I spit, "Stop the car, I want out."

He was angry and intent on getting me home. As he turned the corner, I opened the door, threatening to jump out. He slowed down but wouldn't stop. I remembered watching people jump out of cars on television, and as I looked down at the road, I made the huge mistake of deciding to jump. He immediately stopped the car, jumped out, threw me back into the car, and drove on. At my house, he quickly brought me inside, and immediately departed.

My mother ran to me when she heard my whimpers. She took me to the shower and stepped in with me, helping me clean up and remove the debris from the scrape on my leg. As tears rolled down my cheeks, I apologized to her for being so stupid.

I was surprised to hear her remark, "Oh honey, you're just in love."

I knew she didn't like Barry, but she was not one to give advice. Instead, she told me a story about her life.

"I fell in love with a man I had been dating for four months and I was head-over-heels in love with him. Then I found out he was married," she said.

I wanted to know more. My mother seldom talked about her past. "How did you feel about that?" I asked.

"When he told me he was married, I was devastated. I ended the relationship immediately, but it was a very difficult time for me," my mother explained.

She grabbed a towel and started drying me off. That was the end of the conversation. But what she revealed to me was enough to keep us bonded as a mother and daughter.

It was around that time that my mother went to the doctor complaining of constant, heavy vaginal bleeding. She was checked into the hospital, where they ran tests. They found dysplasia, showing very early signs of cancer cells, and decided to perform a full hysterectomy the next morning. In the 1970s, this procedure was common, especially if the woman had completed her childbearing years. After the operation, my mother was prescribed Premarin, a type of estrogen, which she stayed on well into her 90s. I cooked and helped with the chores while my mother was in the hospital. I cleaned the house until it was spotless just before she came home.

By this time, I had been dating Barry for over two years. I asked my parents if they would give me permission to take birth control pills. Because I was under 18 years of age, I had to have my parents' permission to get a prescription.

"What? No!" screamed my father. "You should not be having sex!"

"Dad. We've been dating over two years. Are you going to tell me that after dating Mom for six years you never had sex?" I reasoned.

"Absolutely not!" exclaimed my father. "We never had sex before we were married, and you shouldn't either."

My father proceeded to lecture me about "abstinence" as I pretended to listen.

In 1971, Barry pressured me to ask my parents if we could have a wedding over Easter. I had turned 17 the summer before my senior year in high school. Barry didn't want to wait for my graduation, but my parents insisted. They allowed us to get engaged, and I started planning a beautiful wedding for the following summer. Barry stewed over the delay; he didn't like my parents dictating what we should do with our lives.

One morning, I woke up with an upset stomach that I thought was the flu. I often felt a sudden urge to run into the bathroom to throw up. My mother was aware of what was happening with me, and noticed that my breasts were swelling.

"Susan? Is it possible that you're pregnant?" my mother asked.

I grew pale.

"No!" I insisted.

"Well, maybe," I conceded.

My mother went with me to the doctor for the pregnancy test. She closed her eyes in disappointment when the results came back positive and insisted that I be the one to tell my father. On the car ride home, I fidgeted, trying to figure out a way to tell him. He could be so explosive at times, and I was afraid.

When he got home from work, my mother blurted out before I had a chance, "Susan's pregnant!"

My father's jaw dropped in disbelief and then he sputtered, "In eight months she'll be swelled up like a balloon!"

I decided to go to my room and wait until the news had settled with him. After a few hours, my mother came and got me.

"We want you to know we will support you. If you don't want to marry Barry, you don't have to. We'll help you raise the baby."

But I was engaged and wanted to get married. Although we'd been dating for three years, I knew I wasn't emotionally ready to get married, but the fact that I was pregnant finalized the decision. My mother arranged the wedding in just two weeks. She took me to Reno to buy a wedding gown, but as I began to look at the white dresses, she approached the bridesmaid dresses and insisted I wear blue because white should be reserved for virgins. I thought that was ironic, because even though she didn't want me to tell anybody I was pregnant, a blue dress would clearly send that message.

I honestly didn't care what my dress looked like. I got married in a blue minidress with a blue veil, and my maid of honor wore a similar yellow dress.

In those two weeks before I got married, my mother also decided that I needed to learn how to clean house and wash clothes. I felt like she was punishing me and became resentful, though when I moved out of her home into my own, I soon realized that the floor behind the toilet didn't automatically clean itself. When I messed up a rug, it didn't automatically straighten itself out. I was also miserable and pregnant, which didn't help my mood.

My marriage to Barry wasn't exactly a storybook, happily-ever-after existence. When he came home from work, instead of a cheerful wife greeting him at the door with dinner on the table as he expected, I was clinging to the toilet with dry heaves. He became irritable with me and I cried at the slightest upset. I didn't realize at the time that my highly emotional state was due to my pregnancy. I was still attending my classes at the high school, and I felt like my life was over before it had even started. I tried to communicate my feelings to Barry, but he didn't comprehend and always turned the conversation around to be about him. I learned early on that it was best to keep silent.

Barry got a job out of town and I decided to move back in with my parents so I could walk to school. My mother was excited to have me back home, and complained that I had moved out way too soon for her satisfaction. I went back to our shared home when Barry came home on weekends and returned there for good after graduating from high school.

It was early in the morning that I woke up with a strong, deep lower back pain. I started having contractions often, so I called my mother. She asked me how far apart the pains were, and I told her about every two minutes. She screeched, "You had better get to the hospital, now!"

Before I could tell Barry to get ready, I felt warm water gushing down my legs. My water had broken. Barry drove like a mad man, bumping over railroad tracks and swerving erratically, while I gritted my teeth and held on for dear life to the car door. By the time we got to the hospital, my contractions were becoming more urgent. The nurses immediately put me in the bed's stirrups and called the doctor. The head nurse, looking like a savage bulldog, sat at the end of the bed, preparing to be the one to deliver the baby if the doctor didn't arrive soon. I would have been afraid of her if I hadn't been preoccupied with my own situation.

One hour after we arrived at the hospital, my child was born. The doctor scuttled in just before I delivered. The bulldog nurse asked me later how I had stayed so calm.

Without hesitation I said, "My mother told me to try and relax and that is what I concentrated on."

I realized how that must have sounded. I was 17 and looked 13, but I noticed a look of admiration and maybe a touch of sadness in that bulldog face.

My daughter Rebekah was the most beautiful baby I had ever seen; I held her in my arms and felt a strong maternal love. Everything about her was perfect; her tiny hands and feet, her great big dark eyes. I took great pride in her; she was my comfort. I learned to cook and clean along with taking care of my beautiful baby.

After the birth, I again moved back in with my parents for a week so my mother could help with the baby. I took to mothering naturally and immediately felt comfortable taking care of my baby, although my mother may not have thought so. I'm not sure if she was challenging me or if she thought I was too young to make a good mother, but once, while I sat on the couch with Rebekah in my arms, my mother came over and grabbed the baby from me. She was getting ready to change Rebekah's diaper when I calmly strode over and took her back. I let my mother know I was in charge, and she never challenged me in that way again.

On a hot August day, while carrying my baby down the hall, despair came crashing down on me. I started crying uncontrollably while cuddling my baby, smothering her with kisses, and mourning not being able go out with my friends or go to college. I mourned the carefree lifestyle I once had. I felt the responsibility that had now changed my life forever, and I told myself that it was my daughter's turn now.

CHAPTER 11

Red Bluff, California

"Susan? You didn't tell me who to call, or anything. My number here is [my phone number]. Can you give me a call? I can't call anybody. I don't know anybody's phone number."

***

Barry and I moved our mobile home from Susanville to Red Bluff and my parents soon followed us, to be nearby. They bought a house and settled in. My mother liked that she lived closer to me and could visit often even though she never offered to babysit, and I never expected it. She did, however, call me often to see how I was doing, and to chat.

By this time, Jim was living in Chico, California as a single man playing lead guitar in bands and becoming a luthier in his own business.

Barry and I started building a house on a parcel of land my parents bought for us. He wanted to build everything by himself or, better yet, with me by his side. He bought a hand-held auger so he could dig a well. He insisted I help by pushing on one side of the auger while he pushed the other. I don't know how he thought I was helping. When he pushed, my feet came flying off the ground and around I would sail, hanging on for dear life. We ended up hiring a professional well digger to finish the job. My mother laughed when I relayed the story of me trying to dig a well.

I encouraged Barry to get his contractor's license and work for himself. He was quick at figuring the math required for production, exceptional at deciphering blueprints for building houses, and skillful at constructing just about every feature in a house, but he was terrified he wouldn't be able to pass the test required to obtain a contractor's license. He asked me to take the test in his place, and partner in business with him. I kept encouraging him until he went to a school and passed the contractor's license test for himself.

Even though he had his contractor's license, Barry took me with him every time he had any business to conduct. I was familiar with construction lingo and had a knack for understanding what was needed and how to communicate with the construction loan officers or the escrow officers. Barry often asked me later to explain what they were talking about. It didn't occur to me at the time just how insecure and incompetent he felt around these people.

I didn't want to be a construction worker, but Barry became more demanding of my help. He insisted I work by his side, even when I became pregnant with our son. Rebekah happily played with her little friends outside while I was required to either keep Barry company or help him build his houses. During this pregnancy, he seemed to want me to do even more physical labor. I lifted one end of the heavy rafters with him and carried them around, balancing them so he could nail them up.

When I was five months pregnant, we decided to move from the trailer park where we were living into our unfinished house.

By the time I was eight months pregnant, our house was ready for sheetrock, and I hoped to have walls before the baby was born. It was difficult for me to hold on to the edge of the sheetrock, and whenever I dropped the corner I was holding, it broke. Barry would curse and throw the hammer around, breaking even more pieces. We finally devised a way to carry the sheetrock by using a little red wagon to help me steer my end.

I woke up one night with a strong back pain and told Barry I needed to go to the hospital. When we got there, the nurses settled me into a room and told me I wasn't far enough into labor to go to the delivery room. After a little while, they checked on me and asked me how I was doing, and if I was having labor pains. I told them I wasn't having pains, but I could feel my baby moving down the birth canal. I asked to be put in the delivery room. Fortunately, they did what I asked without question. I didn't have any pain until the last 15 minutes of delivery. Two hours from the time we got to the hospital, our son Matt was born.

When we got home from the hospital, I took stock of my situation. Somehow, I was expected to take care of our newborn son and three-year-old daughter in an unfinished house. The sheetrock was hung, but the walls weren't finished. I had a bathtub, but no sink. I carried plastic tubs of hot water to the dinette table to wash dishes and sterilized baby bottles in the electric skillet. The yard was a mud pit in November. Barry wore high boots to carry each of us out to the car, so we didn't have to wade in the mud.

There was an occasion when one of our neighbors turned us in to social services. I was washing dishes in my little washtubs when two social service officers mucked their way to the door. I let them in, knowing their muddy feet couldn't do much damage to my clean cement floors. They had heard that Matt had diarrhea, but that wasn't the case. When they asked me where he was, I promptly said, "He's in the closet."

They looked startled, and then concerned, until they went into our bedroom and saw the shirt closet with no doors. The bassinet fit perfectly. Matt was clean and sleeping peacefully. I enthusiastically showed them the rest of the house, babbling on about what the house would look like when it was finished. I was especially proud of the rock fireplace that covered one whole wall. They saw Rebekah taking a nap, also clean and looking peaceful. My house was probably cleaner than most of the homes they inspected, even with cement floors. I never heard from them again.

Barry came home one night, excited about an advertisement for the sale of a laundromat business. He wanted to make more money, and he thought this was the answer, but I talked him out of it, saying there were better ways to make money. Later, he bought several candy vending machines and distributed them around town. It was my job to pile the two children in the car, fill the machines, and collect the money. I stopped by my mother's house one day, but wouldn't go inside. When she came out to the car, she realized why: the children sat in the backseat with sticky fingers and purple faces from eating the candy. She laughed and brought that memory up many times over the years.

I never let my mother know how unhappy I was. To her and others we looked like the perfect family. Handsome, successful husband, pretty wife, and two beautiful children. We went to church every Sunday and faithfully paid our tithes. But, despite appearances, Barry and I were growing further apart, and he started going out with other women. At first, it felt like a knife stabbing me in the heart; I cried until there were no more tears. There were times in the middle of the night when I suddenly sat up in bed and knew he was with another woman. At those times I thought my heart was going to break, but exhaustion eventually took over. I found that I could only go through so many heartbreaks until my heart started to harden.

As I tried harder to keep our marriage from falling apart, Barry found ways to lash out at me. He criticized my clothes, my body, especially my smaller breasts, and threatened me with divorce if I didn't have breast implants. He criticized the way I cleaned house and the sex we had. I tried not to take his criticisms to heart because, deep inside, I knew better.

No matter what I tried, Barry got angry with me and left, sometimes for weeks at a time. I was initially devastated. One night in bed I grew so frustrated that I grabbed him by his hair, tilted his head back, and cried out, "Nothing I do pleases you! I hate you!"

We both were shocked. I had never lashed out at him before. He got out of bed and got dressed, and, just as he was leaving, I cried out, "If you leave, don't come back!"

He looked back at me and hesitated, just for a moment, before leaving.

I didn't know what to do, so I called my mother. She immediately came over, even though it was after midnight. I was pacing the floors and was so furious, I started hyperventilating.

She tried to reason with me, saying, "Susan, if you don't calm down you are going to make yourself sick!"

She didn't know the extent of my pain. I had never shared with her what Barry put me through and how many nights I spent alone at home, crying. I knew if she knew the truth, she would want me to leave him and I was not ready to do that.

Barry may have left for weeks at a time, but he always came back. He started becoming bolder by writing business checks for his visits to brothels. He once wrote a comment on a check stub that he knew I would read: "Fun, fun, fun!"

The mental cruelty was harder on me than the actual act of infidelity. I knew he was trying to make me feel inferior and it started to have a negative effect on me. His constant criticism about how lazy I was, how unsexy I was, how I didn't try hard enough to please him;

it all wore on me. When I cooked one of his favorite meals, he called it slop and sometimes used it as an excuse to leave the house. I felt trapped.

When I stopped loving Barry, I started to despise him.

Barry confessed one evening that he wasn't happy and wanted a divorce. A part of me was relieved; I found an attorney and started divorce proceedings. I moved in with my parents. It was a temporary solution because my mother, concerned that I would get used to my parents supporting me, told me I couldn't stay with them long-term. She didn't want me to go back to Barry; she wanted me to become an independent woman and find a way to support myself and my two children.

Barry moved out; I moved back into the family house and started going to real estate school, so I could have a profession of my own. It seemed like a natural fit since I knew everything about building a house, from the blueprints to the final inspection. I had worked around construction since leaving high school six years earlier.

A peaceful feeling came over me and for the first time I started thinking of life without him. I sold the vending machines while we were separated because they didn't make much money. I was busy studying for my real estate license and had plans to work for a female real estate broker who wanted to employ me. I passed the test easily and was getting ready to go to work. Though I felt vulnerable at times, I was getting comfortable with the idea of being a single mother.

When Barry realized how happy I was without him, he started coming by the house more often. Getting down on his knees he begged every night for six weeks for me to take him back. He informed me he was just trying to punish me—for what, I didn't know—and decided he didn't want the divorce. One night, he caught me in one of those vulnerable moments and once again got down on his knees and begged me to come back to him, painting a vision of a new life with a move to Sacramento. I relented and said we could try again.

Immediately, I felt sick to my stomach and tried to back out, but he talked me out of it, convincing me that this time he would change. Of course, he didn't.

CHAPTER 12

Sacramento, California

"Uh, Susan? Please give me a call down here at the hotel or motel. I don't know where I am. Will you please?"

* * *

My mother was disappointed that we were moving to Sacramento. She liked being around, and spoiling her grandchildren, but she supported our decision and started making plans to move closer to us. She was concerned but accepted that Barry and I decided to try mending our marriage.

When Barry and I moved to Sacramento, we bought a small house to live in temporarily until we could build a nicer home. I didn't know, but when we bought the house, I was pregnant with our third child.

It wasn't long before Barry started the verbal abuse again and left for weeks at a time. I was relieved when he went away and miserable when he came back. My only solace was my two children and then the third when she arrived—another beautiful daughter. We named her Amanda.

After Amanda's birth, I had surgery to prevent any more pregnancies, and developed an infection that totally incapacitated me. I was in so much pain that I couldn't stand up straight, much less walk. I crawled around whimpering, unable to pick up Amanda or carry her around. Barry was unsympathetic to my pain and begrudgingly carried me back and forth to the bathroom when he was home. I went to the doctor, who gave me antibiotics, but wouldn't prescribe pain pills. I took the antibiotics faithfully, down to the last pill, but was still in acute pain.

When my parents came to help, the tension between my mother and Barry was obvious, though she tried to hide it from me. My father's eyes welled with tears when he saw me struggling. He knew how debilitating pain could be and didn't like seeing his daughter in such a condition. My mother brought my baby to me and then went about cleaning or cooking meals. One day, as I lay on the couch watching my mother vacuum, I realized it was the ordinary moments I missed the most: the simple act of walking around, of picking up the baby, of doing everyday tasks around the house.

After a week, Barry asked my parents to leave. My mother barely looked at me as she left me alone to figure out how to solve this predicament. I understood the problem my mother had with Barry, but she knew how much pain I was in. She knew I couldn't walk. She knew I could barely crawl. I was upset that she was leaving me, essentially by myself, to care for a baby, a three-year-old, and a six-year-old. I truly wondered how I was going to manage.

It turns out, Rebekah was my savior. At the age of six, she helped me with bottles and kept watch over her brother. Eventually, the pain subsided, and my body slowly healed.

Years later, my mother brought up this time in our lives. Why did she want to revisit this subject?

I sighed and said, "When you left, I didn't know how I was going to manage."

Her eyes welled with guilty tears as she asked, "Why didn't you ask me to stay?"

I sympathized with her and answered, "I didn't want to force you to stay if you needed to leave. I understood your dilemma with Barry."

We never brought up the subject again.

Barry and I didn't get along any better in Sacramento than we did in Red Bluff, and we were still heavily in debt. I was responsible for paying the household expenses from our checking account and he chastised me if I mentioned our money problems. I paid small amounts on each bill to get us through the month, then went to bed holding my stomach and worrying how we were going to make it through. I learned how to stretch meals to last more than one night. Barry got angry and went to the store to buy potato chips, ice cream, and junk food that only he ate.

He came home from one of his long absences and confessed that he had been with another woman again. As if I didn't know. He stood, looking pitiful, and waited for me to respond, wanting to evoke some emotion. But by this time, I was beyond caring what he did.

I looked at him and casually said, "Well, go and get it out of your system so we can get on with our lives."

His eyes opened wide in disbelief as he stood there with a look of shock on his face.

Wanting more of a response from me, he said, "I'm unhappy. I want a divorce. I know a divorce attorney."

Without emotion, I replied, "Okay, you get the attorney this time."

"Well, I want to think about it," he said.

That familiar lonely, nauseating feeling was surfacing again, and I needed to get away from him. I decided to go to Red Bluff to visit my parents. I needed a distraction, and even though I didn't tell my mother about our problems, I enjoyed her company.

Unexpectedly, Barry showed up at my parents' house and wanted to go camping. We gathered up the children, ages six, three, and six months, and headed out to a lake about three hours away. About halfway there, I noticed that my three-year-old son didn't have his shoes with him. I didn't know how Matt was going to walk around on pine needles barefooted. Barry and I got into a discussion about whether to stop at the store before going to the campsite, which was what Barry wanted to do. Because it was getting late, I suggested we set up camp first before it got dark and go back to the store later. He suddenly became enraged and accused me of always siding against him.

I was drained. We had been married for over seven years and his rages weren't new to me. After trying to change the subject and break the mood without success, I went silent. Sitting in the truck with three small children hovering around me, I contemplated what the weekend was going to entail. His moods could go on for days and I knew we were going to have a miserable weekend. When we got to the campsite—he passed by the store—Barry jumped out of the truck and started throwing the camping equipment.

"Just take me and the children back to my parents," I seethed.

I was beginning to get a headache. Barry gruffly threw our luggage back into the truck and we started the long trip back to my parents' house.

He finally broke the silence by asking, "Why are you always picking fights with me whenever I want to go somewhere or do something?"

I thought back to what it was I could have said to start the argument in the first place. It finally occurred to me that he would have found any excuse to get upset with me. I remained silent, sighing to myself.

It was late when we arrived back at my parents' house. Barry threw our luggage onto their lawn and left us there. My parents heard the squealing of tires as he peeled off and came out to help me with the luggage. My mother looked at me with surprise, but I said nothing. She sensed my mood and left me alone.

The next morning, on July 4th, I went back to Sacramento. I took the children to the fireworks that night. It was after midnight when we got home because the car overheated in the parking lot and I had to shut the engine off and wait for it to cool down before I could start it again.

Barry had been home and left again. He didn't come home until five the next morning, when I heard him thrashing around and realized he had made a bed on the couch. I went to the living room so we could talk. He said he was very unhappy and wanted a divorce.

For a while, he came home around 5:00 every morning and slept on the couch. I continued to wash his clothes, and if he were home, he ate with us, though it was stressful and tense between us. I didn't know at that time that Barry wasn't about to help me financially. He filed for divorce, and this time I knew I would go through with ending the marriage.

I was in a state of shock about what I was going to do. I hadn't made any money in real estate, and I had no idea how I was going to support myself and three children. For over a month I wandered from room to room, feeling depressed, not wanting to deal with even simple tasks. I didn't call my mother to talk to her. She didn't know the extent of what was going on because I didn't know what to say to her. I knew there was nothing she could do anyway. I tried to be cheerful around the children, but they sensed my state of mind.

While this was happening in my life, my parents decided to move to a senior mobile home park in Rocklin, a little town near Sacramento. Before they moved, my mother had asked me if I wanted them to move in with me. She knew I needed financial help, but I couldn't imagine living with my parents in my tiny house—or any house, for that matter. I needed my independence and was hopeful that I could find employment and support my children. I was grateful that I lived in Sacramento, where there were more opportunities. Even though I had my real estate license, I was too young and inexperienced to make a steady income and was worried that I would have to leave the children too often to show houses and build my profession.

My parents were supportive of the divorce, but my debts were too huge for them to help much. They decided to buy a new car and gave me their old Buick and, occasionally, money for gas. They bought shoes and three sets of clothing for my children. That was a huge help to me.

Barry came home one night to pick up some of his tools from the garage. He started in about what a terrible wife I had been, and how all of this was my fault. I sat silently and listened for a while, letting his words sink in. He paused and looked at me with accusing eyes. Then I calmly told him that he was a bastard, surprising myself. I had never used such strong language before. He became furious. He threw a glass of water toward the television, leaving a gash in the wall. He threw the lamp off the table and knocked over furniture. He picked up the couch, threw it down, and barely caught it before it landed on the baby, who lay on a blanket on the floor. Realizing what he had almost done, he left.

Barry's attorney sent me the divorce papers to sign. There was no problem with the division of property, even though most of it went to Barry. I wasn't upset that he took what he did. I was relieved to move forward with my life, out of that stressful relationship. I would rather have lived in poverty than go back to him. I was happy to keep the house I was living in, and the little furniture he left behind. He left me the proceeds from the sale of a house he had built in Red Bluff that was still in escrow. My mother gave me two overstuffed chairs so I at least had living room furniture, and I set up a little radio on a bookcase.

We were still heavily in debt, and even though I was supposed to receive money from the sale of the Red Bluff house, which I planned to use to catch up on bills, I started to worry about my future. The divorce papers specified child and spousal support, but I found out through my next-door neighbor that Barry had never planned on helping me financially. My neighbor told me that Barry wanted me to beg him to take me back and said he was planning to "bleed me dry so I would have to go on welfare." My mother was furious when she heard that and offered to pay for a consultation with an attorney. I accepted her generosity with relief.

Shortly after seeing the attorney, Barry and his brother came over to the house to pick up some of his tools that were still in the garage. Barry was enraged upon learning that I had seen an attorney. I sat at the kitchen table as he walked past me and through the door to the garage. He came back with a roofing hatchet. With a determined look in his eyes, he smashed it into the coat closet and then swung around, hitting the wall in the hallway. Still enraged, he went outside and flung the hatchet into the side of the house and then into the side of my car. I sat motionless, afraid to move a muscle. His brother watched me in silence, and although he said nothing, I could see the concern in his eyes.

My mother didn't know what to do. She hadn't been completely exposed to this side of his sociopathic nature before. I hadn't confided all the demeaning and humiliating conditions I had weathered. I didn't want her to know how much pain I'd endured because of my decision to marry him. I was embarrassed and thought it was my burden alone to bear.

When he wasn't being physically intimidating, Barry often tried to upset me. One demand was, "Since you have the three kids living with you, I think I should have one of them."

I played reverse psychology. "Okay, which one do you love the most?"

He had no answer. I knew he did not want the full responsibility of raising his children, and would never follow through.

I paid our monthly bills from the savings account I set up from the sale of the Red Bluff house. I'd started looking for a job when my attorney offered me a minimum wage, part-time position until I found other work.

On my first day of work, I woke up early with a nervous stomach, excited to start my new job. I got the children up, fed, and dressed and took them to a neighbor who said she would babysit for me. It was a foggy morning as I drove the large Buick my parents had given me down the long country road to the main street that would take me to work. Suddenly, the car started dragging and I knew I had a flat tire. Barry had put a nail through my tire again. I pulled over to the side of the road, not knowing what to do next. A large semi-truck saw me and stopped to help.

As a result, I was late on my first day of work. I walked into the office, breathless from running up the stairs, and apologized for being late. A beautiful blue-eyed blonde woman looked back at me, smiled, and said not to worry.

She introduced herself, "I'm Lil."

She was 24 years older than me and we became best friends.

There was an attorney in the office who had just passed the bar exam and I started working for him as well. Not having typed for seven years, I was a little rusty, but it didn't take me long to get back into the swing of it, and I was thankful for the work. My part-time job as a legal secretary eventually became full-time, and that was the beginning of my career in the legal field.

Everything was going well at work, but in some ways, little had changed at home. Late one night, Barry came to the house, intoxicated, and threatened to rape and beat me to a pulp. I hadn't changed the locks on the house. He tore the bedroom phone from the wall and threw it aside. He then turned and pinned me down on my bed and yelled and screamed at me. He shook me by the shoulders and slapped me with his hand a few times. I cried, but I tried not to fight him. Instead, I went limp, hoping he would stop. He grabbed me by the shoulders again and threw me over the side of the bed. My head came down hard on the floor and I went into shock. He put his hands around my throat, squeezing so tightly I couldn't breathe. My heart was pounding so hard I could feel it up in my throat. I didn't think he wanted to kill me, but I was afraid he might lose total control.

He finally loosened his grip around my throat, and I managed a whisper, "You don't know what you're doing."

He took his hands away and got up. I heard him walk down the hall, and when he got to the kitchen, I heard him dial the kitchen phone. Just before he left, he ran back to the bedroom to tell me he had called the police and I could talk to them if I wanted. I lay on the bed, unable to move for some time. Whether or not he called them, I will never know.

I was thankful to be alive. Death had never been so near to me before. After a time, I managed to get up. I stumbled into the kitchen, noticed the handset of the phone dangling against the wall, and put the phone to my ear; when I knew nobody was on the other end of the line, I hung up. I tried to pull myself together, get my thoughts unstuck. I felt numb and unable to comprehend what had just happened. My body started shaking involuntarily.

I walked back and looked in on the children. The girls were in their bedroom sleeping peacefully. When I looked into Matt's bedroom, I saw him lying in his bed with wide-open eyes, the reflection of the hall light, shining from them and making them sparkle with fear. My heart was touched, and I welled up with tears. I went in and scooped him into my arms and rocked and sang to him for a long time. My voice was shaky, and my body felt weak, but somehow, we managed to give each other comfort.

Because Barry had never done anything physical to me before, I decided not to press charges. And then, one night a few weeks later, I heard him come into the house. I was in the back room putting the baby to bed when I heard breaking glass. I ran out just as he left and noticed his framed contractor's license in the trash can. I was afraid he would come back, so I packed up the children and went to a friend's house for the night. My mother would have willingly let me stay with them, but I did not want to involve my parents any more than I had to.

The next morning, as I drove the children to the babysitter, I saw Barry walking along the side of the road. He had a vacant look in his eyes that frightened me. I dropped the children off at the babysitter's house and went to my house so I could quickly change clothes for work. As I walked back to my bedroom my stomach started to curdle. I saw that my clothes were strewn all over the room and drawers had been emptied. An iron had been thrown against the dresser mirror, causing it to shatter, and crushed glass was scattered all around. I drew in a quick breath and ran into my bathroom to get ready for work. All my creams and cosmetics had been emptied into the sink. I slowly turned back into the room and started to take inventory.

It was then I noticed blood splattered on all the walls. It was seeing his blood that frightened me the most. Every piece of my clothing was drenched in it. The smell nauseated me.

I put my hand over my mouth and let out an involuntary scream. I bent over and grabbed my stomach—I was going to be sick. My body started trembling and I turned to run. On the way out, I noticed a pair of scissors stabbed into my bedroom door, with dried blood that had dripped down from them.

My body was suddenly lithe and my mind alert. As I ran out of the house, I shuddered as the thought crossed my mind: what would have happened had I been there when he came back. And then I wondered what would have happened if the children had been there to see this.

As I jumped into my car, I was in a full panic. My only thoughts were to get as far away as I could, as fast as I could. I passed Barry again. This time he was farther up the road and he had a look of despair on his face. There was a stop sign, but I didn't stop, so afraid that he might catch up and try to jump into my car.

When I got to work, I called my babysitter to tell her what was happening. She offered to help me clean up. I managed to work until noon and then went home to clean the mess before the children saw it.

My babysitter's husband came by to help, got sick, and had to leave. I noticed that every piece of clothing had been cut with scissors. I managed to salvage three items plus the clothes I was wearing. I found a blood-stained note he had written telling me how terribly I had treated him and that, although I was "no good," he still loved me. There were fingerprints of blood at the bottom of the note, as though he was signing it with his blood. This time I took him to court, and he was ordered to pay me child support and the cost of replacing my clothes. He did neither.

Barry disappeared again, leaving me his truck, his business checkbook with some signed blank checks, and a note saying I could have everything. I didn't see him again for four months. He called me once from Florida, charging me for the long-distance phone call. He wanted to know if I wanted him back because if I didn't, he wasn't ever coming back. I told him I wasn't going back to him and then I took the opportunity to ask him why he had destroyed all my clothes.

He laughed and said, "Because I love you."

I responded, "Well, that's a sick love." And even though I didn't say it, the thought of going back to him nauseated me.

So, I was left with everything, including the bills. With monthly expenses amounting to more than my salary, my only hope was to liquidate as much as possible. My savings account was beginning to deplete from paying off our debts and monthly bills. My goal was to keep my house. My attorney suggested bankruptcy, but I was too proud. I had enough money in savings to get by for a while and an unfinished house under construction that Barry left for me to deal with.

My attorney was impressed that I was willing to finish the house, but what he didn't know was that I knew exactly what to do. We went to court to get permission for me to receive the remainder of the construction loan so I could finish construction and sell the house. As I sat in the box next to the judge in the courtroom, she turned to her side and looked down.

Speaking directly to me she asked, "You can finish this job?"

"Yes, I can finish construction of this house," I replied.

She looked at me in disbelief, seeing what to her looked like a tiny teenager even though I was all of 25 years old and mature for my age.

She asked me again, "You can finish this house?"

"Yes, I can finish this house."

And then I went on to explain exactly what needed to be done, using contractor's terms that I had learned through the years from helping Barry. She must have been satisfied because she gave me permission to finish construction of the house. She also gave me sole custody of the children, allowing him reasonable visitation rights.

I supplemented my minimum-wage income from my savings account watching my funds dwindle down. I began to wonder how I was going to manage and went to consult a social service officer to see if I qualified for welfare.

I owned a house and had too much money in the bank to qualify for financial support, but I did qualify for food stamps to help me buy groceries. It was humiliating to accept welfare food stamps, so I went to grocery stores far from where we lived. We went from eating rice and beans to eating steaks. The first time I prepared the meat, Matt, who was four years old, asked, "Mom, is this what a steak looks like?"

In the meantime, I had to deal with the house Barry abandoned that was still under construction. It was one thing for the judge to give me permission to finish construction—it was another to actually do the work.

It took four months to finish the house. A neighbor down the street, who became a good friend, helped me. We worked evenings and weekends until I was able to put the house on the market to sell. It was difficult because of all the stress I was under and the nauseous feeling I got in the pit my stomach every time I stepped foot in that house. I felt as trapped finishing that house as I had felt in my marriage and had to force myself to go over and work on it. After we finished the work and the house passed all the inspections, I put the house up for sale.

Barry came back to Sacramento and tried to take back his truck and the house I had finished, which was already on the market. He sat in another truck across the street, watching me clean the truck he had left behind so that I could sell it. I knew he would default on the payments if I gave the truck back to him and the creditors would come after me. He, of course, bitterly accused me of taking everything from him and informed anybody who would listen just how terribly I treated him.

In 1978, the market for selling houses in Sacramento was slow. It took a year for Barry's house to sell. Escrow closed two weeks before Christmas—the best present ever. When the house finally sold, I was able to get out of debt. It had been a year of scrimping and scraping, and not having money for food or clothes. A heavy weight lifted from my shoulders. It felt as though I had been through a dark, rough storm and the sun was beginning to shine.

Barry started seeing his children sporadically, seemingly with the goal of trying to spoil any plans I might have made. Sometimes, he told me he was going to pick them up on Friday night and bring them back on Sunday; they eagerly packed their bags and impatiently waited for him to pick them up. Eventually, enough time went by that it became obvious that he wasn't going to show up. I hated what he was doing to them, and to me. I tried making excuses, telling them he loved them. Other times, he took them on a Friday night and brought them back a few hours later. I bitterly wanted to tell him they were his responsibility for the weekend and to get a babysitter, but when I saw them standing on the porch with their little eyes peering up at me, my heart melted, and I enthusiastically received them back. I was furious with him for playing games, and using his children to do so, but there wasn't much I could do about it.

Barry eventually started taking the children for an occasional weekend. On one of those occasions, when he brought them back, we argued over money. Our divorce was final by this time, but his tools were still in the garage. He wanted me to give him the $100 I received for a tool I had sold. I refused because he had never paid child support. Looking back, I should have just given him the $100 or, better yet, not sold the tool in the first place. It would have turned out for the best in the long run. He became so upset he started pointing his finger and shouting, and I asked him to leave.

He left in a huff, and I slammed the door shut and locked the deadbolt. I had pent-up anger after many years of his mental abuse but locking him out was a huge mistake. I heard him start to kick the door down. I realized he was going to come after me. I ran towards the phone, but before I could dial the first number, Barry had knocked down the door and was by my side. He grabbed me by the hair and threw me up against the kitchen cabinets. I felt the handle of the cupboard jab me hard in the tailbone. He grabbed me by the hair again and threw me on the kitchen floor, swinging me from side to side while shouting threats. It felt like a lifetime passed before he finally left.

I don't remember how long it was before I looked up. I saw Rebekah, who was only seven, looking down at me. She held Amanda in her arms and had Matt by the hand. Looking concerned, she asked me if I was all right. Before I could get up, Matt ran outside. I slowly got up, trying to reassure Rebekah that I was fine. About five minutes later, my parents walked through the door. Many years later, Matt told me he thought I was dead.

I hadn't had time to pull myself together and fell into my mother's arms crying. My father became furious and said he wanted to buy me a gun, to which I replied, "He would probably take the gun away from me and kill me with it."

I was able to appease my father by telling him he could get me a bat.

Around this time, Rebekah became very frightened and concerned about me, after spending the weekend with her father. Barry had told her that he had hired someone to kill me. She was also worried that he was going to take her and her siblings away from me. I tried to ease her mind by telling her he would never be able to take her away, but there wasn't much I could say about the supposedly hired killer.

Barry called not long after; he asked if we could get together and talk. Even though Barry rarely saw the children, I thought he was concerned for them. Not knowing yet that I was wrong about that,

I agreed to meet him in a parking lot, presumably to discuss the children.

After some persuasion on his part, I got into his car. I became concerned when he started the engine and began driving. He described to me how he had barely survived the four months he was gone.

I pondered what he said for a while and asked, "So, do you want my pity?"

He responded, "No, I don't want your pity."

"So, you have the ability to make 10 times more money than I do. You left me with three children to support and aren't willing to help. And you're telling me how hard you have it?"

As he drove, he became aware that his manipulations no longer worked on me. He also began to realize that I had no intention of going back to him. He had lost control of me. He put his foot to the gas pedal and started running stop lights. I knew if I said anything more it would provoke him, so I sat and said nothing until we were back in the parking lot. He dispassionately looked over at me.

In a quiet monotone he said, "I'm going to kill you along with 10 other people and then I'm going to kill himself."

I couldn't believe he would really do that.

"What about the children?" I asked; "what do you think will happen to the children?" I was trying to get him to empathize or at least think through and consider the consequences of his actions.

"Welfare will take care of them."

I tried desperately to think of a way to escape without provoking him.

He looked over at me and said, "I'm sorry. I would never kill you."

Then, he softly asked, "Would you give me one last kiss?"

I felt nauseated at the thought of kissing him. He must have seen the expression on my face and knew.

He looked at me with a desperate expression and said, "I have a shotgun at home, and I'm going to use it on myself."

I knew he was trying to emotionally blackmail me.

Softly I whispered, "Do whatever you think you need to do."

I grabbed the handle and opened the car door. I stepped out, too frightened to give it any further thought, and quickly walked over to my car. I was afraid to even look back as I jumped inside my car, started the engine, and drove directly to Lil's house for comfort.

I fell into her arms sobbing, "What if he really does kill himself? I will never be able to forgive myself." Lil held me tightly.

"He'll never do that." Her soothing voice was comforting.

Shortly after this incident, Barry got married. He must have been planning this before we met at that parking lot. I was relieved and yet somewhat surprised. I was hoping he would finally leave me alone. Instead, for years I often got obscene phone calls and nails in my tires. Sometimes I came home to find my electricity turned off at the main breaker. For the next 20 years, I received occasional calls in the middle of the night with either heavy breathing or silence on the other end. The last I heard, Barry moved back to Susanville, where he lives to this day.

As for our lives, it was comforting to know I could always go to my parents' home nearby in Rocklin if I felt lonely and needed company. Almost every Sunday, I packed up the children and went to visit them after their church service. My mother either cooked dinner or they took us out to a fast-food restaurant. After moving to Rocklin, my parents had joined a bowling league, and they taught their grandchildren how to bowl. In the summer, we all went swimming in the clubhouse pool or sat in the spa.

Coming from small towns, my mother and I were not used to the large shopping centers in Sacramento. One time we went shopping and forgot where we had parked. Rain poured down while we went from parking lot to parking lot, looking for the car. We were soaked and frustrated, and at one point we stopped, looked around, and then looked at each other. We threw our heads back and pealed with laughter, then doubled over and stumbled around holding our stomachs. We pointed fingers at each other, blurting out how we looked like drowned rats.

When my parents took us out to dinner, they usually asked me where I wanted to go. I knew that, to them, a nice restaurant was a chain that served mediocre food. I usually suggested Mexican, or someplace that served good hamburgers. Wherever we went, my parents waited for me to order and then ordered the same thing. I was still in the position of making the decisions for everybody, although I didn't even realize this was happening until years later. I didn't understand it. Had they always had problems making decisions or was this something that they felt was my responsibility as their daughter? Whatever the reason, I became the decisionmaker.

If I weren't visiting my parents, they came to me, usually on Sundays. During one of those visits my father confronted me and in an imploring voice told me that I needed to take care of them. I was 25 years old, going through a horrible divorce, and trying to balance raising three children with work and discovering life as a single mom. Barry still refused to pay child support and saw his children only sporadically, so that I could never rely on him. I wondered how I was going to raise three children by myself, much less take on the responsibility of caring for my parents. I was an emotional mess and didn't need any more responsibilities. I excused myself and went into my bedroom. I needed to think. I took a deep breath, calmed myself down, and told myself I could do this. I rationalized it worked in my favor as well. Their companionship would help get me through these tough times. I knew without Barry's financial help, it was going to be difficult, and I was grateful for my parents' emotional support. I then went back into the living room and sat next to my father.

I looked at him for a moment before saying, "I will be here to help with whatever you need."

This seemed to please him.

Despite hard times, I was so thankful for the new direction of my life. It felt like I had been released from a long prison term and I was now a free woman. Lil and I went out almost every Friday night. We started going to a local nightclub because neither of us had money to spend and we loved to dance. It was a great place to meet and socialize with friends. Lil and I started West Coast Swing dancing and even though most of the people I met were 15 or 20 years older, I felt comfortable around them. I thrived on this feeling of freedom that Lil's friendship and dancing at the club provided in order to bear the responsibilities I faced the rest of the week.

My mother formed the habit of calling me right before I left the house, to ask what I was doing with the children. Of course, I had a babysitter, but she tried to make me feel guilty for leaving them.

"Poor things—you tell them if they get scared to call me."

"Okay, Mom."

"You be sure to tell them that."

"Okay, Mom."

On the other hand, if I decided to stay home for a while, she told me I needed to get out and meet someone. There just seemed to be no pleasing her.

At one point, my father was scheduled for open-heart surgery, one of many surgeries he underwent due to his chronic heart disease. He was a veteran, so most of his surgeries were performed in a veteran's hospital located at the Presidio in San Francisco. I always went with my mother to keep her company through the long, torturous hours of waiting. The hospital was beautifully designed, and we sometimes sat in one of the atriums that overlooked the bay while we waited.

This time, Barry showed up. He was supposed to be in Sacramento watching the children, but he said he had left them with the babysitter and decided to come to the hospital. He flirted with me and was on his best behavior. He reminisced about the good times that we shared. I had the distinct feeling he still hoped he could win me back, even though he was already remarried. He knew he had lost all control of me, but when I treated him kindly, he thought I was still in love with him. I wanted to get along with him for the children's sake. They needed him to act like a father.

Years later, I realized he was probably a sociopath or someone whose attitude includes manipulation, aggression, and lack of empathy for others. A sociopath's defining characteristics are a profound lack of conscience with a flaw in a moral compass that usually steers them away from heeding common rules and treating others decently. This behavior is usually hidden by a charming demeanor, which describes Barry in every respect.

After surgery, the doctor let us see my father in the recovery room; Barry tried to follow us.

I abruptly stopped him, saying, "Absolutely not! Dad would think he had died and gone to hell if he woke up and saw you hovering over him."

My mother threw her hand over her mouth and suppressed a giggle.

When my father was out of recovery and settled into his room, he asked me to remove his partial dentures from his mouth. He was still groggy from surgery, and for some reason my mother had left the room and headed for the car so we could go home. I didn't know exactly what to do, so I went over to him and tried to remove his partials. I had a rough time getting them out, so I crawled up on the bed, straddled him, and pulled with all my strength, wary that someone would come into his room and wonder what I was doing. I was still unable to remove the stupid things. I finally gave up and left. When

I caught up with my mother, I told her what I had done and how I had done it. She laughed until I thought she was going to pass out. Of course, when she laughed liked that, I laughed with her until we were so giddy, we could barely walk. When she was finally able to pull herself together, she told me I was pulling on his real teeth.

My father recovered from his surgery and was back at home when I started to notice his personality was changing. I'm not sure if it was all the surgeries he had been through, the medication he was on, a restriction of blood flowing to his brain, or all the above. Sometimes he argued with his grandchildren as though he were also a child.

My mother had a hard time adjusting to my father's increasing limitations. She had to take over the driving, while my father threw up his hands and yelled at her for the way she drove. Once when I was following them in my car, I saw my father's hand gestures and could tell he was yelling, while my mother stoically drove the car. It was funny to watch, but I knew she wouldn't see the humor.

It was during this time that I got a call from my cousin, Judy. I was in my bedroom when the phone rang.

"Hi Susan. This is your cousin Judy from Texas."

"Judy! How nice to hear from you! How are you?"

"I'm fine but your father and my mother got into a huge argument the last time they talked on the phone. It's terrible and I don't know what to do about it." Judy's mother was my father's sister who lived in Texas.

"Well, they're always fighting," I replied.

"Yes, but the fighting is getting worse. And another thing. Your mother is mean. She called my children fat the last time they visited us in Texas." Knowing my mother, I had no doubt that was true. With irritation I defended her.

"Well, Judy, I don't know what you want me to do. She's my mother. The last time I saw you, I was 12. I haven't talked to you in over 20 years. I don't even know you. I love my mother and I think it's inappropriate that you call me to complain about her."

Judy quickly hung up the phone and I never heard from her again.

After the phone conversation, I sat on my bed and pondered our conversation. I could understand her frustration, but I did not need another person to worry about, especially someone I barely knew. It was enough for me to have to deal with my mother.

As I sat on my bed, I looked around the room. Our house was becoming too small for the three children, especially with Matt as the middle child between his two sisters. He usually shared a room with his younger sister because they got along, but he was getting to an age when that was going to be inappropriate. The two girls were opposite in nature and couldn't share a room, so I set out to find a four-bedroom house, finding one in a newly developed neighborhood nearby. The house was under construction, and I was set to move in after a few months.

I'm not sure why, but my father wanted to buy my old house from me. My mother, on the other hand, didn't want the house, but she wouldn't stand up to my father. Even though my mother was used to deferring to him, she loved playing the victim so she could punish him for decisions she hadn't approved. I sat her down once and told her I wouldn't sell them the house if she didn't want me to. She balked but told me to go ahead and sell it to them. My father was elated. He loved the little place, and that was the house they lived in until after his death, my mother living on there until she was forced to move to an assisted living community in the last few months of her life.

Once, when I had my parents over for dinner, my mother came to me with tears in her eyes. She told me how difficult it was for her to deal with my father. I sympathized with her; I could only imagine what her life was like.

During one of my parents' visits, my father came into the house disgruntled. He complained because my mother had backed out of the driveway while his foot was still dangling out of the car door. He kept yelling, "Nadine, stop, stop!" She ignored his screams and continued to slowly back out. Silent acts of rebellion like this were the only ways my mother could say No to my father. It was typical of her passive-aggressive nature.

There was another instance when my parents were coming back from visiting their friends Bill and Edith in Little Rock, Arkansas. I always took them to and from the airport. In those days you could go right up to the gate and meet the passengers as they came off the plane. As the passengers filed off, I waited for my parents to come out. One of the passengers came up to me and asked, "Are you Jim's daughter?"

"Yes, I am," I said, while thinking, what a gregarious guy, he makes friends wherever he goes.

The passenger exclaimed, "Oh, we're so glad you're here! He was so worried that you wouldn't be here to meet them."

I was shocked and indignant. What could my father have been thinking?? I had never flaked on them! The minute he walked out of the passenger boarding bridge, I accusingly asked him why he would say such a thing. He impishly smiled and said he had tried to call me earlier, but I wasn't home.

From there, we went down to baggage claim. My father asked my mother to stay with the carry-on luggage. For reasons of her own, she immediately shuffled off to another area of the airport, leaving me no choice but to stand watch over the carry-on suitcases.

As the luggage came around on the conveyor belt, my father, who had been told not to lift anything over 10 pounds, spotted one of their suitcases and leaned over to pick it up, but he was too weak. Before my eyes, I saw him awkwardly stand up on the carousel to try and get a better hold of his suitcase. He managed to get one hand on the suitcase with both feet on top of the carousel. Swaying a bit and trying not to lose his balance, he finally fell in with all the luggage as it moved around the carousel. He raised his free hand, trying desperately to grab on to the edge, when a strong young man grabbed my father's arm. He lifted him off the carousel, placed him securely on the solid floor, then snatched my father's suitcase and placed it beside him. At my father's direction, the young man also retrieved my parents' second piece of luggage as I stood there, horrified, watching the scene unfold before me. A woman came up from behind and sympathetically asked, "Are they yours?"

She must have been watching the whole scene play out. All I could do was nod in the affirmative. I noticed my mother standing at a distance with a smug smile on her face.

The couple my parents had flown to visit, Bill and Edith, were good friends whom they met in El Paso, Texas when I was a young girl. The men were in the military together, and it was the same place and time we met Reese and Marvin. Like Reese, Edith quickly became one of my mother's best friends and they, too, were a pair of mischievous troublemakers. They reminded me of Lucy and Ethel in the television show, *I Love Lucy*.

When they were young women, they painted their long fingernails red and smoked cigarettes. They kept in touch over the years, and even though they never again lived in close proximity to each other, when their husbands retired, they reunited every couple of years, for about six weeks at a time, to travel somewhere by car, or hang out at each other's homes.

During one of those visits, my mother drove and chatted with Edith as they came to a stop at a red light. Deeply engrossed in conversation, they suddenly became aware of cars honking behind them on the busy street. Curious about what the commotion was, they got out of the car to get a better look around them, then looked at each other and started laughing, realizing the honking was at them, for not driving when the light turned green.

When Edith and Bill visited my parents, the four of them often traveled somewhere, always by car. After one particularly long day of driving they decided to find a place to stay for the night. They stopped at a hotel near San Francisco, and Edith and my mother went in to rent a room. The attendant stoically asked how many hours they needed. Startled, they both snorted and then started roaring. They reached the car with tears in their eyes from laughing so hard. They were obviously in the wrong section of town. This was one of my mother's favorite stories to tell as she reminisced about their time together.

Once when Edith and Bill were visiting, I invited the four of them to lunch; I knew of an English pub down the street from my office that I thought Edith and my mother would love. But first, I wanted to show them around where I worked because by this time, I was working for a justice of the state appellate court system.

I had worked as a legal secretary for six years when I applied for a job as a central staff secretary for the Court of Appeal, Third Appellate District. When I got this state job, I knew that I would be able to raise my children comfortably and retire with a pension. It was a tedious job, typing for attorneys; because I had a legal assistant certificate, I was overqualified, but it got my foot in the door. After 18 months in that position, a justice on the appellate court invited me to work for him because his assistant was about to get married and move away. I jumped at the chance, and this was the workplace I wanted to show off a little to my parents and their friends.

My mother praised me to her friends, but she never shared this praise with me, or gave me any indication she was happy for me. I never imagined at the time that perhaps she might be intimidated. As I ushered the group around the office, Edith and my mother made a point to appear as if they were unimpressed, though they'd put on their finest clothes for the occasion. With their fancy fur coats, red lips, and long red fingernails, they put on superior attitudes, with their heads held up high, faces unsmiling, acting pompous and ostentatious as if they came from wealthy families. When the justices, who were warm and friendly, shook their hands, Edith and my mother looked down their noses with smirks on their faces. I noticed a gleam in some of the justices' eyes. The husbands, on the other hand, were gracious and unpretentious, which helped make up for the embarrassment I felt. Despite their act, my mother and Edith were giddy when they informed their friends of their exciting adventure.

The four of them, my parents and Bill and Edith, were very comfortable with each other. I was expected to go over for dinner frequently when Edith and Bill visited. Sometimes I found them all napping; other times, I found that Edith and my mother had painted their husbands' toenails red while they were asleep.

Because I knew that Edith loved to dance, I invited the group to go to a bar that featured country swing dancing. Edith was so excited that when I got to my parents' house to pick them up, she was happily dancing around the kitchen. My father came out looking spiffy, wearing a cowboy hat and boots, but my mother refused to go out with them unless he took off that "silly" cowboy hat. My father looked disappointed as he took off his hat; Bill suggested they stay home, and my mother agreed. I was about to leave when I saw the look of disappointment cross Edith's face. I reached over and gave her a quick hug and whispered in her ear, "Let's just the two of us go."

Her eyes lit up as she mischievously whispered back, "Let me get my coat."

Bill shrugged when he realized that Edith was going out with me and decided to join us. My parents stayed home.

The three of us danced and laughed and had a great time. While men eyed Bill and Edith, they nervously asked me to dance. They thought it was strange that I was out dancing with my parents, and asked me about it. I didn't want to constantly explain the situation, so I shrugged and explained they wanted to come. I really didn't care what they thought. After dancing until after midnight, we went out to breakfast at an all-night diner. As we ate, the men I had danced with started straggling in one by one. They laughed and waved when they recognized us.

Even though my mother could be difficult—criticizing my father's hat and staying home—she could also be a lot of fun. I got a call from her one evening, barely understanding her chortling. I loved her contagious laugh.

"Susan?"

She was laughing so hard she couldn't talk, causing me to laugh with her.

"I was getting ready to take the garbage can to the curb, but your father insisted he would do it." My father was getting weaker and shouldn't have been toting something so heavy.

"Your father—" laughing so hard by this time she barely made sense, "Your father tried getting the garbage can onto the curb when it started to tip."

I could imagine her wiping tears from her eyes.

"He was trying to get it upright, but the lid came open and he fell in headfirst. He was hollering while upside down in the garbage can!" She was in a full roar.

Still having trouble containing herself she sputtered, "The neighbor had to come over and pull—pull him out."

We laughed together for quite a while.

My father often bore the brunt of my mother's teasing. Nonetheless, he took it in stride and worshipped her. Once, at Christmas, I took my father shopping to buy my mother's gift. They liked shopping at the Military BX nearby, so that's where we went. I saw a bright fuchsia jacket and teasingly told my father we should buy that. His eyes immediately lit up in agreement. I now realized why my mother wanted me to go shopping with him. I inspected the jacket carefully and casually reasoned that she probably wouldn't like it and we moved on.

In 1994, my 77-year-old mother needed cataract surgery. I went with my parents to the hospital so I could keep my father company and help afterward. As we waited at the hospital, I noticed him start to fidget.

"Why is it taking so long?" he asked.

I tried to comfort him, saying, "It's going to be all right. This is how Mom and I felt when you had all of your surgeries."

He looked at me with tears in his eyes.

"I had no idea how hard it was for you two on this end."

When we got home, my mother went to the bedroom to sleep. My father said that while I was there, we should get the tires changed on their car. I didn't want to leave her, and I knew better, but he was so insistent that he needed to get those tires changed as soon as possible, that I went with him. When we finally got back home, my mother was sitting on the couch, arms crossed and perched lips, with a look that could kill. I felt guilty for leaving and chastised my father for thinking the tires were so important that we had to leave her home alone. He sheepishly looked away, shrugged, and admitted the tires could have waited.

I stayed with them that evening and made dinner. My mother felt better and came to the table to eat with us. While admiring an oil painting of a vase with flowers, I told my mother, "I have always been drawn to that painting."

She smiled at me.

"Have I ever told you about that picture?"

"No. What about it?" I asked.

"Well, after your grandmother died in the crash, I found a tiny picture of that vase with flowers in her purse. I took it to a German artist the first time we lived in Germany and asked him to paint an oil painting of it for me. When I die, you should have that painting."

I now have that painting hanging in my house. I am even more drawn to it, now that I know the history.

My mother's baby picture.

This comes from a collection of pictures I have of my mother as a child. Here she is posing with her brother.

A very cute picture of my mother as a little girl.

My beautiful mother at the age of 30.

This is a passport picture of my mother and Jim.

My mother, father, and Jim the first time they lived in Germany.

My father with Duke next to him, my mother holding Pepe, and me holding a baby chick. Notice how Duke was eyeing that chick!

My mother and father standing in front of our house in El Paso, Texas.

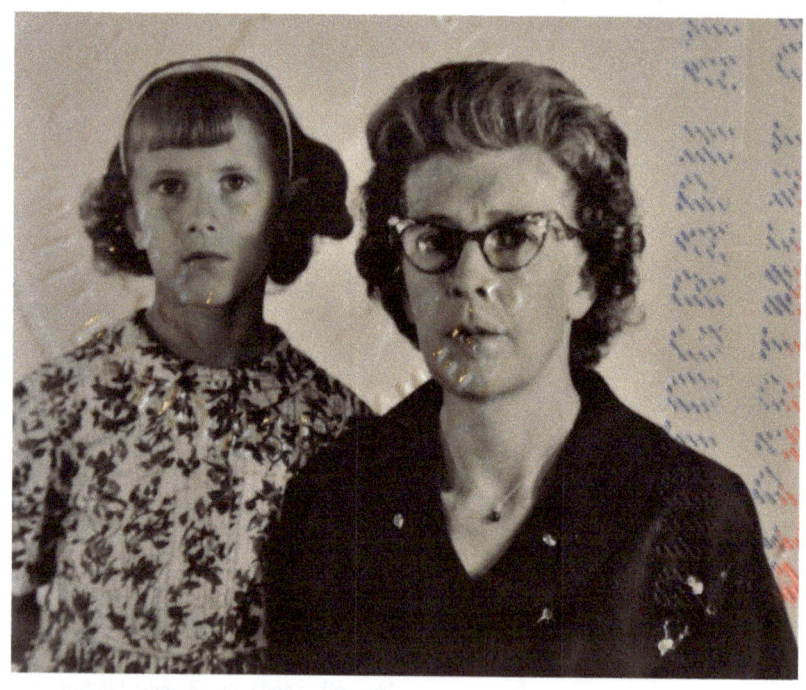

A passport picture of the two of us. We were obviously in disagreement about something. Neither one of us is happy.

A family picture taken in 1963 when I was 10 years

My mother loved to bowl and played on a team for many years.

Me in my blue wedding dress.

My mother and father.

She looks like she is contemplating something.

My mother was the organist at her church until she was well into her 90s.

Sam captured my mother gambling in Reno. She usually won something.

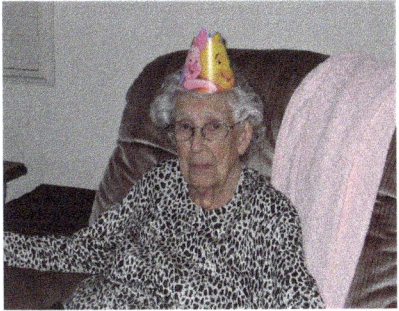

This picture was taken before she was diagnosed with Alzheimer's. The smirk on her face was typical when she was not happy about something, like posing for the camera.

My mother making gravy.

My mother posing with Sam and me. She became very emotional when she first saw me walking down the stairs.

I never saw my mother flirt with anybody like she did with Sam's Uncle Teto.

Sam snuck this picture of my mother at Amanda's wedding. It was such a good picture of her, we used it on her funeral announcement.

Here I am with my mother in her tiny apartment after she was diagnosed with Alzheimer's Disease.

My mother after her diagnosis. This picture captures the blank look she was starting to get as her disease progressed.

CHAPTER 13

Heaven or Hell

"Susan? I'm having a terrible time trying to get this telephone to do what I have wanted it to do. I just can't seem to get it tonight. I wish I could get ahold of you. I'm trying [my phone number] and I'm going to hang up and try to ring it again. If you can hear this, give me a call."

* * *

In 1983, I had been divorced for four years and was about to turn 30 when I met Johnny. I was still a legal secretary at the start of our relationship and even though I didn't make much money, I was content and happy. I thought I was ready for a stable relationship and was looking for someone to share my life with. We met at the bar that I often went to on Friday nights with Lil. He was handsome, with beautiful hazel eyes that twinkled when he smiled. He asked me to dance and I was immediately attracted to him, even though I saw many red flags at the beginning of our relationship.

It was confusing when he called me sporadically, asking me to go out with him. I knew he was attracted to me and wondered why so much time went by before he would call me again. He finally admitted he was in another relationship that was ending. I told him to call me when he was single again. He called me shortly after that, to tell me he was free and that he would like to have a relationship with me.

He fell in love with Matt and Amanda, but Rebekah, who was 12, did not warm up to him and there was strife between them throughout the entire relationship. My mother immediately liked Johnny because, as she put it, he was a spiffy dresser, wearing designer jeans and expensive shirts.

I soon learned that he had a short temper and yelled and talked over me. It was frustrating, and after a few years, I started talking over him and yelling back. I didn't like myself with him and doubted I could ever marry him. Our relationship consisted of either getting along beautifully—heaven—or arguing over any little thing—hell. There wasn't ever a moment I felt relaxed or content. He was either sweet and complimentary or he was yelling and insulting me.

Johnny's short temper got him into a shouting match with my father over Johnny's dog Gable, who happened to be the sweetest dog ever. We had invited my parents over one evening and the three of them sat in the living room while I made dinner in the kitchen.

My mother came running into the kitchen in a panic.

"Susan? They're fighting. I mean, they are really fighting!"

I stopped and listened to the raised voices in the living room.

My father said something to the effect of, "If your dog bites one of my grandchildren, I will kill it!"

To which Johnny responded, "If you kill my dog, I will kill you!"

Johnny's dog had never bitten anyone, and I couldn't imagine why they were even having this argument. They settled down when I went and stood in the living room. Embarrassed, Johnny came to me later and apologized.

I had been dating Johnny for five years when he rented out his house and moved in with me. I thought it would help me decide whether I wanted to stay in this relationship. I figured it would make or break us, but now, I had no escape from him.

He came home from work, turned on the television, put his feet up, and waited for dinner. He expected me to cook, clean house, and wash his clothes. I was surprised because I expected him to help me, since he had been living alone most of his life, cleaning his house and doing his own laundry. I didn't mind cooking and cleaning, but did mind washing his clothes and it wasn't going to happen. Mostly what I didn't like was his attitude. His behavior was extremely sexist.

"Johnny, I work a full-time job, as you do, cook the meals, and now you expect me to wash your clothes? You need to wash your own clothes," I explained.

"Your job isn't as important as mine," he retorted. "You know that, don't you?"

"No, I work to support my family and have done just as well as you. My job is just as important as yours. You have to wash your own clothes," I replied. "I'm not going to."

He looked shocked and hurt. Because I was a woman, he felt he could sit back and do nothing even though he had been taking care of himself for years.

"You're just lazy," he said in disgust.

I started to get that trapped feeling with him, even though we weren't married. When my parents asked if my children and I could join them on a trip to Oahu, Hawaii, I enthusiastically took them up on their offer, thinking to have fun and relax while I pondered my next step in this relationship.

My parents booked a hotel with adjoining rooms. They slept in one of the rooms, and my children and I slept in the other. Each child took turns sharing my bed, which meant I didn't get much rest. Eventually, my mother noticed bags under my eyes and offered to give their other bed to one child at a time, so I could sleep alone, and more soundly.

We all decided it would be fun to take a tour around the area by bus. We were getting ready to board and I was concentrating on getting the children settled when I looked around and saw my mother standing alone.

"Where's Dad?"

My mother threw her arms up and shrugged, "I don't know!"

I sighed. I was exhausted. I closed my eyes for a moment, then opened them and looked directly at my mother.

"Look, you keep track of Dad, and I will keep track of my three kids."

She stared at me with exasperation.

"I can't do that! I can't keep track of him!"

With a resolved tone in my voice I said, "I'm getting on the bus." As I boarded, I saw him bound around the front of the bus, snickering.

We stopped for lunch later at a fast-food restaurant. My children ran to find a table as I stepped up to the counter and started to order.

My father interrupted, "I'm the man of the family—I should be the one to order."

I stepped aside. He started floundering and then stopped and stood still for some time, wistfully looking over at me. I knew he was embarrassed, so I quickly stepped up and placed our order.

While it wasn't exactly relaxing, we all had a great time, despite my father arguing with the children now and again. When we flew home, it was late, and we still had to drive from San Francisco to Sacramento. I drove, with my mother in the passenger seat and my father in the back with the children. One minute, they were laughing and talking excitedly about our trip, and the next, my father started yelling that someone had taken his straw from his soda. They got into a loud tiff, and my father let out a whoop that caused me to jump.

Exasperatedly I snapped, "Stop! If you don't settle down right now, I'm going to pull over!"

Instantly there was silence, and I drove home in peace. My mother sat silently.

When we got home, I was exhausted. Still, the trip to Hawaii had put enough distance between me and my relationship to give me a chance to ponder my life with Johnny. I realized I couldn't live with him if I wanted to keep my sanity. He scolded me about something unimportant while I sat on the bed.

Resolutely I looked up at him and said, "I'm committed to my family, but you are dispensable. You need to leave."

I helped him find an apartment and fronted the deposit until he could move back into his house, which he had rented out. It was difficult at first because he didn't want to let go of the relationship, and I thought I was still in love with him. In the end, though, I knew I had done the right thing.

CHAPTER 14

Another Mistake

"Did I get you, Susan? I wasn't sure 'cause it was such a quick message. I called [my phone number]. This is Mom. Give me a call, please!"

* * *

After my breakup with Johnny, I went to counseling. I was tired of allowing the wrong men into my life and tired of being miserable. I made up my mind to choose joy and wasn't going to let a man make my life miserable again. My children started teasing me that I would never remarry.

I had been divorced from Barry for 14 years when I met Alex. My mother thought Alex was very handsome and approved of the relationship. Alex was tall and strong, with deep brown eyes. To some, like my mother, he was handsome, but I wasn't initially attracted to him. But I thought, maybe, he was what I needed: someone to enjoy life and have fun with. He was all of that at first. He wanted to marry immediately, but I resisted, suggesting that we wait at least a year. I wanted more time for us to get to know each other.

So after a year, we had a small, simple, outdoor wedding in a private park. It was beautifully set against rolling hills with lush green grass and old oak trees scattered about. I wore a calf-length, elegant eggshell dress, and my two daughters and Alex's daughter looked stunning in their peach-colored dresses. Matt was handsome in the tuxedo he wore to walk me down the aisle and give me away. We crossed a quaint little bridge that arched over one end of a small lake. There was a slight breeze, and the sun was warm and luxurious as it washed over our skin. We had access to the clubhouse where Alex's mother made a scrumptious meal of chicken mole, rice, and beans as a wedding present for us.

The wedding was about to start when my mother noticed that Alex's mother was still in the kitchen laboring over the hot stove. My mother would have none of it and, marching into the kitchen, took Alex's mother by the arm, announced that the wedding was about to start, and they weren't going to miss it.

Because the wedding was small, I didn't need a large wedding cake, but my mother insisted on having a groom's cake, which is nothing more than an additional cake to feed the guests. Her friends Bill and Edith from Arkansas were there, where it was customary to have a groom's cake. We didn't need it, but I wasn't going to argue with her. She picked out and bought a large sheet cake that remained untouched.

It was during this time that my Uncle John and his wife came to visit my parents. Unexpectedly, after almost 40 years had passed, he called my mother and said they were traveling to California and wanted to stay with her for a couple of weeks to try and mend their relationship. Coincidently, Jim's daughter, my niece, was four years old.

I wanted to warn Jim to watch his daughter carefully around Uncle John because of what he did to me when I was her age, but when I got to his home in Chico, I froze.

Instead, I told Christy, his wife, "I don't trust my Uncle John around your daughter. Watch her carefully."

That was all I had to say.

My mother invited us all to dinner during the visit. I was nervous. Doubt started to settle in, and I questioned if I might have been mistaken about him. But the minute I walked into the house and saw him, I knew. He was the man who molested me when I was four years old. I couldn't stand to be in the same room and could not bring myself to hug him. I looked over at his wife and had the distinct feeling she knew what he had done to me, and probably many others.

As we stood in line to get a plate of food, somehow Jim's daughter ended up behind me with Uncle John behind her. I stepped out of line and gently guided her to step in front of me while glaring at him. The rest of the evening went without incident and Alex and I left early. Uncle John and his wife left the next day and I never saw them again.

Alex and I settled into marriage, having fun with friends, making travel plans, and starting a life together. I was surprised when, a few months into our marriage, Alex abruptly quit his job and started college, without discussing it with me. I became resentful.

"Alex, when I married you, I thought we were entering into a partnership. I didn't expect to have to start supporting you," I logically explained.

Alex looked at me for a moment and said, "Isn't this what couples do in a marriage? They support each other."

"Yes, and maybe if you had waited a few years and discussed this with me first, I would totally support you. But you didn't. Did you know you were going to do this before we got married?" I asked.

"No, I just thought we were here to support each other, and this is what I want to do," he replied.

This was starting to have a familiar ring. Did I attract men that wanted nothing but be taken care of? He listened awhile longer while I explained that I did not want to be the sole income earner. He nodded his head in agreement. He said he understood. But he continued his schooling, staying out later and later. When we went out together, I noticed him overtly flirting with other women. Our relationship took on a completely different quality from the year before we were married. I woke up in a cold sweat one night and reached over to an empty space next to me. I knew he was with another woman. It was the same feeling I got when I was married to Barry. My night remained restless, and the next morning I started shaking. As I showered, I pondered what I wanted to do about this marriage.

I asked myself, *Is this what you want out of life? No! Do you see light at the end of the tunnel? No!*

I knew I needed to get out of the relationship for my own sanity.

The next day, Amanda and I were on our way to shop for Christmas presents when I noticed Alex's car parked on the side of the road. Thinking he was having car trouble, I pulled over in front of him. A young woman jumped out and started running.

I went over to his car in bewilderment. "What was that all about?"

He shrugged.

"She's one of my classmates in school."

I saw through his lie, went back to my car, looked at Amanda, and said, "I need to get all my Christmas shopping done today because I'm not going to feel like shopping later."

She looked at me thoughtfully, then mentioned that when she looked in the rearview mirror, she noticed his wedding ring on the opposite hand.

Later that evening, Alex came home. I asked him about his ring, which, I noticed, was now on the correct finger. He shrugged.

I contemplated my words carefully.

"I think I'm going to start acting like you."

"What do you mean? You aren't me."

"Well, maybe I should be. Maybe that is what attracted me to you in the first place. I think I'm going to start acting just like you."

He looked down for a moment and quietly said, "I want a divorce."

I nodded my head in agreement.

"Okay, I'll start the paperwork."

With a pained look in his eyes, he covered them with his fingers and started to cry. I sat still, feeling a numbness creep over me. I looked over at him in time to see him spread his fingers far enough apart to see through them. When he saw no reaction from me, he quickly removed his hands from his eyes and stared tearlessly back at me.

That was the end of my second marriage. A friend of mine at work called it the "quickest divorce in the West."

CHAPTER 15

Finally Getting it Right

"Susan? This is your mom. I'm down here at the hotel again. Please give me a call. Would you please?"

* * *

I met Sam in 1995, the year before my father died. Sam was a struggling grad student, getting his master's degree in biomedical engineering. My mother wasn't initially impressed with Sam because he mostly wore worn-out T-shirts and red Teva sandals. In other words, he wasn't a spiffy dresser, or at least she didn't see that side of him in the beginning.

Sam had never been married. I was a single mother of three. We met in a little English pub located in downtown Sacramento through a girlfriend who wanted to go there to see her ex-boyfriend. I saw Sam standing at the bar having a beer and was immediately attracted to him. He looked younger than he was, and I thought to myself, *If I was only 10 years younger!*

A man I had no interest in came up to me and started flirting.

I whispered in Sam's ear, "Would you mind pretending to be my boyfriend tonight? I am not interested in this man and I don't want to hurt his feelings."

There was a twinkle in his eyes as he answered, "No problem."

I learned that while Sam was getting his degree, he was working part-time. Basically, he was a starving student.

I thought to myself, *Too young, no job, no way!*

Later he told me after he learned I had children that he thought to himself, *Three grown children!*

But the attraction was there.

As the night waned, my girlfriend suggested Sam and his friend join us for breakfast. She knew he was a wonderful man and wanted me to get to know him. They accepted and we had breakfast in a restaurant down the street. I sat next to Sam and my friend sat next to Sam's friend. We laughed and talked for a while. As Sam and his friend talked about their lives, I felt the heat stir between Sam and I, but given my history, I wasn't going to be swayed by a charming breakfast companion. I took my leave of Sam without letting him learn too much about me, and with no plans to get together again.

The next time we met, again at the pub, I paid close attention to how his friends reacted to him. I asked about his parents, whom he seemed to have a good relationship with. I looked into his deep brown eyes and felt a strong charisma pulling at me. We listened to his friend sing in his new band and someone gave me a camera to take pictures. I stood on a chair, looking down at Sam as he looked up at me.

My body seemed to be a separate part of me, while my mind was asking, *Sue, what are you doing?*

But my head was swirling, and I continued to dance the dance. We sat close and looked into each other's eyes, communicating silently that we were attracted to each other. Sam was shy and afraid to make the first move, and I wasn't going to ask him out on a date.

I was still old-fashioned enough to want the man to ask the woman out on the first date.

Just as I was about to give up, he finally asked, "If I asked you, would you go out with me?"

Without hesitating I smiled and said, "Yes."

He smiled and smugly went to the bar, got a matchbook, and wrote his phone number on it. I laughed to myself. He forgot to ask me for my number. I looked at the number, looked back at him, and said, "I'll call you Monday."

We've been together ever since.

CHAPTER 16

A Long Story Short

"Susan? Would you please call Mom? I need some laxatives and I don't know how else to get it if we don't go get it."

* * *

Through all the childhood trauma, challenges with my mother, troubled relationships, and raising children as a single mother, I grew and learned. I choose to regard these experiences in a positive light and today I prefer to think I am wiser and happier.

There is a poem that aligns perfectly with my life. It is titled, "Autobiography in Five Short Chapters" by Portia Nelson.

Portia Nelson was a striking character who was born in 1920 as Betty Mae Nelson and died at the age of 80 in 2001. Born in Brigham City, Utah, she was raised in a Mormon family. She dropped out of college after two years and moved to Los Angeles. She had an interesting life as a singer-songwriter, actress, and author. She portrayed the cantankerous Sister Berthe in *The Sound of Music* in 1965 and the long-running role of the nanny Mrs. Gurney in television's soap opera drama *All My Children*, as well as many other roles throughout her life. She was a cancer survivor, having conquered breast cancer after a mastectomy in 1973. She conquered throat and tongue cancer in the early 1990s. She lost her soprano voice, but she kept singing, in a low husky voice, until 2001 when her breast cancer recurred, and she shortly thereafter died. She wrote hundreds of songs, books, musicals, and animated films which went unproduced and a book of poems titled, *There's a Hole in My Sidewalk: The Romance of Self-Discovery*, where this poem came from.

This is her poem, which I've annotated with notes from my own life.

AUTOBIOGRAPHY IN FIVE SHORT CHAPTERS

Chapter One [Barry—10 years]

I walk down the street.
> There is a deep hole in the sidewalk.
> I fall in.
> I am lost …. I am helpless.
>> It isn't my fault.
> It takes forever to find a way out.

Chapter Two [Johnny—5 years]

I walk down the same street.
> There is a deep hole in the sidewalk.
> I pretend I don't see it.
> I fall in again.

I can't believe I am in this same place.
But, it isn't my fault.
It still takes a long time to get out.

Chapter Three [Alex—2 years]

I walk down the same street.
There is a deep hole in the sidewalk.
I see it is there.
I still fall in ... it's a habit ... but,
my eyes are open.
I know where I am.
It is *my* fault.
I get out immediately.

Chapter Four [Avoiding men]

I walk down the same street.
There is a deep hole in the sidewalk.
I walk around it.

Chapter Five [Sam—over 25 years]

I walk down another street.

CHAPTER 17

My Father's Passing

"I think I left you one. But it's Mom and I'm at [my phone number]. Give me a call when you get in, would you please?"

* * *

The first time Sam met my father, my Uncle Fred was visiting. I called him uncle, but he was really my mother's cousin's husband. My father and Uncle Fred immediately liked Sam and competed for his attention. They competed with each other in the stories they told and engaged Sam in telling them stories of his life.

It took my mother some time to warm up to Sam, though. Frowning, she asked me, "Is there any way you could spiffy Sam up a bit?"

She loved men who dressed nicely and was especially attracted to men in uniforms.

"Maybe," I answered. "But I love him just the way he is."

Eventually she came to appreciate him and bragged to her friends about his intelligence. She learned that Sam came from an upstanding family and knew how to dress when the occasion presented itself. Sam respected my mother, but always came to my defense when she belittled me.

Sam loved my father. He patiently sat and listened to my father's stories for hours. He encouraged my father to tell stories about his military experience, until my father got nervous and said he could no longer talk about it. There was a moment immediately after one of my father's surgeries when his head was clear, and his intelligence shone bright. The moment didn't last long but Sam was able to see the man my father used to be.

My father was very gregarious, and never met a stranger. He could stand in a line and make friends. Anyone who met my father liked him instantly; maybe it was his Texas drawl that drew them in. He loved to tell stories and told them to us many times over. We could finish his stories, yet now I'm unable to remember them. I need him here to remind me what they were. He often got into arguments with my children as if he were a child himself. He had been sick for many years and had blocked arteries in his neck, causing oxygen restriction to his brain. Because of that and all the surgeries and medications, his personality changed, and he could no longer communicate in his effortless, articulate manner.

In 1996, a year after Sam and I had started dating, my father's health started deteriorating rapidly. I suspected that he'd reached a point at which he wanted to die and quietly stopped eating. When I visited their house, I'd see his pills scattered all over the floor; he was throwing handfuls of pills toward his mouth, not caring if they landed in his mouth or not. He began to need help getting around, and it was too much for my mother to take care of him alone.

When I arrived at the celebration of their 49th anniversary, my father was in their bedroom, unable to join the family. I went to see how he was doing. In the dim light I could see his small, weak body under the covers. I gently laid myself down next to him.

"Hi, Dad. How are you doing?"

I could barely see that he was trying to smile. In a raspy voice he managed to say, "I made it."

I knew he meant he had made it to their anniversary.

"Yes, you did!" I said and quietly rose from his bed and slipped into the front room to tell my mother we needed to take him to the hospital.

We had to get the neighbor next door to help Sam get him into the car. They gently hoisted him up and carried him. We took him to the military hospital nearby. Two doctors asked my mother and me to join them in a small office, showing us his advance health directive that requested he not be resuscitated if his heart stopped, or he stopped breathing. They wanted to know how the family wanted to proceed.

It was very hard for my mother to tell the doctors what they could or couldn't do, and at one point she got frustrated and exclaimed in exasperation, "You should know what to do, you are the doctors!"

The doctors looked at us, perplexed.

"Let me try to help," I interrupted.

I looked over at my mother while searching for a way to articulate what the doctors needed to hear.

"Mom, the doctors are required by law to do everything possible to resuscitate him and keep him alive unless you tell them otherwise."

My mother exhaled a long sigh and slowly began to speak.

"Oh. My husband and I have discussed this, and he doesn't want to be resuscitated."

She looked over at me with tears in her eyes and asked, "Am I doing the right thing?"

I reached for her hand and looked directly into her eyes.

"Yes, you're doing the right thing."

My father refused to eat, and while my mother sat in a corner, I tried to hand-feed him, watching with resignation as he spit out the food. At one point the nurses asked him if he was cold. He looked over at me quizzically, as if to ask me if he was cold.

I looked at the nurses and nodded. "Give him more covers."

I looked over at him as he tried to get out of bed, looking at me as he was doing so, as if asking permission.

"Dad, you need to stay in bed," I said, so he lay back down.

It didn't occur to me until later that it had become solely my responsibility to determine what they needed. My father died a week later, in September 1996. At that point, he'd been ill for years and hadn't been expected to live past the age of 60. My parents were married for 49 years before my father passed, just a few months before he turned 81. My mother was 79. She lived alone for another 17 years, until the last 13 months of her life.

At the time of my father's passing, my mother still played the organ for her church and had many friends. She had started taking piano lessons at the age of eight. By the age of 12, she played regularly in her local church. She said her mother volunteered her to play for parties and funerals and admitted she was very nervous when she first started playing. She continued to play the piano throughout her life, switching to the organ when she was an adult. She played the organ for her church until she was well into her 90s. When she quit playing, she used the excuse that her eyes were failing, but in hindsight, it was probably due to mental degeneration.

When my father passed, Sam drove my mother and me to the funeral home, where we were led to a room full of coffins. Without any discussion my mother and I immediately separated and started scurrying around as if we were on a mission. Sam said he was amused as the two of us went from coffin to coffin trying to find the right one for the right price. I finally came to one that was for veterans. It was perfect, with a red, white, and blue interior, and reasonably priced. I asked my mother to come take a look, and she agreed that it was a coffin he would have liked.

We insisted my father have a military funeral. My mother refused to have "canned" music, so they set out to find someone to play "Taps" on a bugle, and seven military men with rifles to perform the 21-gun salute. The men were elderly retired servicemen, and at the last minute one of them got sick and could not attend. As the six men shot their rifles three simultaneous times, nobody seemed to mind the 18-gun salute instead.

Shortly after my father's passing, Sam and I took my mother with us to the local bookstore. Inside there was a small café. I sat my mother down and said Sam and I were going to find what we needed and come back for her. I made sure she was comfortable before I left.

When I came back, she had a large chocolate candy bar in her hand. "Mom, where did you get that?"

"Some older gentleman gave it to me."

I looked over and saw a small group of elderly people sitting in the café.

"Really? Well, did you give him your phone number?"

"No, should I have?"

That was so like my mother, to sit with a stoic look on her face, showing no emotion. She didn't seem in the least bit interested.

I said, "Okay, let's go home."

As we left the store, she leaned into me and declared, "I'm coming back here!"

When my mother envisioned her life alone, I think she hoped she and her dear friend Edith, who she imagined would also be widowed, would visit each other often. That was her backup plan. But after a life of smoking cigarettes, Edith died of emphysema, shortly after my father, so that vision was never realized.

Edith's husband, Bill, came out to visit my mother shortly after Edith died and stayed for three weeks. Her close friends in the church questioned why my mother, a single woman, would allow a widowed man to stay in her home. They did not think it was appropriate and told her so. But she was neither embarrassed nor apologetic. She had known him for many years and considered him a good friend. They traveled to the familiar places they used to visit as a foursome and tried to fill the lonely gap that opened after losing their spouses. Bill, also a longtime smoker, fell ill with emphysema shortly after his visit, the same way his wife had, and passed away.

With Bill's death, my mother was on her own, without the comfort of the friends she had known for so many years. Still, she continued to live her life as always, going places and doing the things she enjoyed. She loved to go to Reno or Lake Tahoe and play the slot machines. In those days there was a lever on the side of the machine, to be pulled down after depositing coins. They were called "one-armed bandits" because most people lost their money. Not my mother. She always won something. She usually played the nickel machine because nickels lasted longer than dimes or quarters, and she usually won enough money to pay for dinner or a hotel room. Every time she got near a gambling machine, whether at an airport or even in a bathroom, she reached into her purse for a coin to play. Sam took a picture of her playing at the Reno airport.

My mother called me often, but she did not seem depressed or lonely. She said she spent more time with her friends and was adjusting well to life without my father.

CHAPTER 18

Changing Times

"I am so turned around I'm upside down. I will give this message one more time. Call Mom when you get home. Bye-bye."

* * *

As my mother was learning to live without my father, my relationship with Sam was becoming solid. My mother and I were going through major changes, not only in our own lives, but also in the way we dealt with each other.

Sam and I sometimes took my mother to dinner with us. We also took her with us whenever we went to visit my brother Jim and his wife, Christy, who lived about 90 minutes away.

One year, Jim and Christy invited all of us over to their home for Christmas, along with Christy's family, so we gathered up my mother and took her with us. Christy told me later that she had made homemade whipped cream, but my mother brought a store-bought container and insisted Christy serve it. We sat around the dinner table, chatting, when my mother said out of nowhere, "You know, there is asbestos in the whipping cream."

The table went silent for a bit. That was bizarre. We picked up the whipped cream container and looked at the ingredients, trying to figure out where she might have even gotten that idea. Her statement made no sense. Was she joking? Not really. She was serious. We mused over it for a while and then moved on to another subject. Upon later reflection, this might have been a precursor to her illness. The rest of the day, however, was uneventful, and we had a wonderful time together as a family.

Sam and I got married in 1999, after living together for four years. We lived in the Bay Area and decided to have the ceremony and reception at the Claremont Hotel, a very elegant venue, but cheaper than most because they had a half-off discount on Sundays. We decided Sunday would be a good day to get married. I had never been married in a long white dress, so I took my daughters and found the perfect wedding dress for me, and bridesmaid dresses for them. Matt was to give me away. Sam's parents came in from Washington, D.C. and generously hosted a night-before rehearsal dinner. Sam's parents are elegant and sophisticated, and I noticed my mother fidgeting as she approached me and nervously asked if she was expected to say anything. I could see how uncomfortable she was.

"Mom, relax and enjoy yourself. You don't have to say anything if you don't want to." Reassured, she elegantly moved through the room with confidence.

The day of the wedding I was dressed and ready for pictures, which we decided to do before the ceremony. As I came floating down the stairs in my beautiful gown, my mother gasped as she threw her hand over her mouth. She looked up at me with tears in her eyes. Embarrassed at her outburst of sentiment, she said, "Sam's father said you cleaned up good," hoping to get a reaction from me.

I chuckled because I had already noticed her reaction.

Our wedding was beautiful, and the day magical. We tried to keep the gathering small; it was mostly family. We ended up with 60 guests—my family of eight, Sam's family, and a few close friends. My mother was relaxed now that she knew she didn't have to perform.

She sat at the table with Sam's single uncle, Teto, and flirted like I had never seen her flirt, before or since. Unfortunately (or maybe fortunately), Teto lived in Washington, D.C. or he would likely have found himself under my mother's spell. Teto reminded me of my father in many ways. Of course, he was nattily dressed for the wedding, but he also was small in stature, and had the same quiet way about him as my father had.

In 2000, my mother's doctor found a large lump in her right breast. He immediately and unhelpfully told her he was almost positive it was cancerous. The surgery was scheduled immediately; the plan was to perform a biopsy that would be tested while the surgery was underway. That way, if it were cancer, they could remove her breast immediately. The doctor asked her if she wanted reconstructive surgery, but she was not interested. To everyone's surprise and relief, the lump turned out to be benign.

In 2004, Sam and I moved back to Sacramento. We bought a house about 30 to 45 minutes away from my mother's. I was unpacking when she called and asked what I was doing.

"I'm starting to unpack my crystals."

"Okay, I'll be right over to help," my mother enthusiastically remarked.

I knew she had misunderstood me. She thought she was going to help unpack crystal drinking glasses, not crystal rocks that I had been collecting over the years. When she got to the house, she looked disappointed as I started unpacking my collection. She grabbed a fragile sea urchin that I had received as a gift. She tried to crush it as I grabbed her hand and pinched her wrist to make her let go. She finally released her grip and instead found a heavy crystal to drop on my beautiful Brazilian maple hardwood floor. I pointed my finger toward the living room and asked her to please go sit down. I wondered to myself what she would have done if there had been crystal glassware to unpack.

It was much easier on me when we moved back to Sacramento. We were able to go to dinner often as a family; going to dinner with us was one of her favorite pastimes. Sam and I would usually pick my mother up and then take her home. One evening after dinner, I asked Rebekah if she would drive her grandma home.

"Sure," she said. "Grandma, do you want to ride home with me?"

"Of course, I do," said my mother.

On their way to Rebekah's car my mother noticed a "For Sale" sign on it.

"Oh, this is such a cute little car," she mused. "How much are you asking for it?"

When Rebekah told her, she looked taken aback.

"For this piece of shit?"

In July 2005, my mother backed her car out of the garage and, as the garage door was beginning to close, suddenly remembered she had forgotten something. She jumped out of the car and tried to run underneath the door before it closed all the way down. She slammed against the door and was thrown backward, landing hard on her back. She lay in pain until a neighbor saw her. The neighbor immediately called an ambulance and then called me.

I rushed to the hospital and found my mother in the emergency room, in extreme pain. An X-ray revealed that she had fractured her right hip. She was 88 years old at the time. The doctor came in and told her that she needed surgery, but he was going to put a pin in her hip rather than do a full hip replacement. Before he left the room, he said that it was doubtful she would ever walk again. She looked over at me, still in pain and with her eyes wide opened.

I waited until he left, bent down close to her, and whispered in her ear, "He doesn't know you very well, does he?"

After surgery, the nurses asked her to rate her pain level on a one-to-ten scale. She looked to me for help. She didn't understand, until I told her they would give her pain medication if she was in pain.

From then on, every time the nurse came in, she pointed her right index finger toward the ceiling and bellowed, "Eight!"

After a week in the hospital, they sent her to a nursing facility for a three-month recovery period. The nursing facility was close to where I lived, so I could visit every evening after work. When she first arrived, she pressed her lips shut and refused to eat. We became concerned that she would get too weak to recover, so I brought her some juicy cantaloupe from home, which I knew was one of her favorite foods. She eyed that cantaloupe until I saw her hand slowly reach over and surreptitiously take one of the slices. She just couldn't help herself even though she still complained bitterly for me to get her out of this place.

She looked at me with menacing eyes and said, "This is what you do to me! Put me in a place like this and throw away the key!"

Completely drained, I scolded, "Compared to your life of 88 years, three months is a drop in the bucket."

I brought her a big calendar and started marking off the days until she would be able to come home. That seemed to help. Out of boredom, she spent most of her waking moments in the rehabilitation room, where they showed her exercises to help strengthen her muscles. Every time I visited, she protested that she didn't like the place and wanted to go home. In an accusatory voice, she mentioned that the lady in the bed next to her had a son who came to visit every day. Did she not realize I visited her every day?

Two months into her recovery, Amanda came out with her nine-month-old daughter to stay with my mother. When I visited, my mother made us all exercise together. She made a remarkable recovery and was walking and running around in no time.

Jim and I got her a medical alert pendant to wear around her neck, but she refused to wear it. I went over to her house and found it on the kitchen counter. I always tried to put myself in her position and wondered what I would be like if my children insisted on my wearing a pendant. I knew that her resistance stemmed from her not wanting us to tell her how to live her life. I came up with the idea of getting her a cell phone to take with her on her walks instead. She loved it and took it with her everywhere. Sometimes she called me just to be able to use it.

During this time, I was able to talk her into setting up a living trust, so her property wouldn't have to go through probate. I told her we could each get one together. My employer, an appellate court justice, recommended a friend of his who was an estate attorney, and we saw her together.

The attorney asked me, "How do you like working for your boss?"

"He is great. I really enjoy working for him."

Suddenly, my mother blurted, "It sounds like a little hanky-panky going on to me."

I wanted to crawl under the table. The attorney and I stopped and stared at her in astonishment.

Clearing my throat, I hoarsely whispered, "I don't think you really mean that, Mom."

She sat there with a smirk on her face until we finished our business. After all that, she refused to put her house in the trust because she said she was afraid I would throw her out into the streets. She didn't understand what the trust was for. It ended up as an unnecessary expense, except for the power of attorney; I was grateful that I had that when she could no longer manage her affairs.

Even though she seemed to be getting feeble, we kept our holiday traditions; I fixed Christmas dinner and she made Thanksgiving dinner.

Around this time, when Rebekah started dating her soon-to-be husband, his mother invited us to her home for Thanksgiving. She asked me if my family would bring a salad, vegetable, and dessert and she would make the rest of the meal. I happily said we would oblige. Rebekah told me she wanted to make a pumpkin pie, so I called my mother.

"For the Thanksgiving dinner, we are asked to bring a salad, vegetable, and dessert. Rebekah wants to bring the pumpkin pie," I said.

"Well, I thought I would make the pumpkin pies," my mother replied.

"Well, Rebekah wants to do that, so can you bring a salad or some kind of vegetable? Maybe your candied sweet potatoes?"

I was trying to get her mind off the pies if possible.

"I'll call Rebekah and talk to her about it," she said.

"Okay, talk to you soon then. Bye," I answered.

Not long after I got a call from my mother.

"Uh, Susan? I'm in a real pickle here. Rebekah is very upset with me and I don't know what to do about it. I called her and told her I was making pumpkin pies for the Thanksgiving dinner. She told me she wanted to make the pies. So I told her well, I'm making pumpkin pies. She got real upset with me and told me not to make the pies because she was going to. What should I do?" she asked.

I laughed to myself thinking, two peas in a pod. They were so much alike.

I thought about what her response would be to me, if I were in her shoes, and answered, "Well, you got yourself into this mess, you get yourself out."

She was silent.

"Why don't you make your candied sweet potatoes or a nice salad?" I reasoned.

"Well, I'll think about it," was her final reply.

On Thanksgiving I brought a vegetable and a salad, and Rebekah brought her pie. My mother brought nothing.

After that incident, my mother tried hard not to upset Rebekah. Normally, they got along well, as she did with Matt and Amanda. Either she called them, or they called her. Each time they spoke, my mother called me immediately after she got off the phone.

"Guess who I just talked to?" she bragged.

I could hear the excitement in her voice as she proceeded to tell me about the conversation.

It was after Thanksgiving that her next-door neighbor, who had remained friends with Barry, came to visit her. He announced that Barry would "take" me back. By this time, Sam and I had been married for several years, and Barry and I had been divorced over 26 years.

My mother frowned and in an aggravated voice questioned, "Why on earth would she want Puss Brain back? What does he have to offer her? She is happily married to Sam now."

We were sitting in her two recliner chairs when she later told me of the conversation. I wanted to reach over and kiss her.

When Rebekah got married, and started having children, she wanted to have Christmas at her house so we could all be there when the children opened their presents on Christmas morning. To my mother's relief, I then took charge of Thanksgiving dinners, while we had our Christmas dinners at Rebekah's house. My mother still had us over on Christmas Eve for her famous chili and cornbread.

On Christmas Eve in 2006, my mother called me late that night and said she was in pain. I knew it must be significant for her to call me. I went over and took her to the emergency room. The triage nurse asked my mother what medications she was on and was surprised at how little medication she took at her age. While they admitted her quickly due to her age, we waited most of the night for them to convey the diagnosis. They discovered she had a right femoral hernia, but surgery wasn't scheduled until the following July. We got home early on Christmas morning and decided there wasn't enough time to sleep, so we went directly to Rebekah's house to open presents, red-eyed and giddy.

To simplify buying family Christmas presents, we created a list we called "The Family Circle," which assigned each of us one family member to buy a gift for each year. One Christmas, Amanda's husband was the lucky person who got my mother. He asked her what she wanted but she refused to tell him. She wasn't comfortable telling anybody what she wanted as a gift. She preferred everyone to figure it out for themselves and not disappoint her. He was at a loss as to what to get her. He persistently asked until she told him she wanted a brick. When she opened one of her presents from him, she got her brick. She laughed in good humor and used it as a doorstop.

My mother decided to take her brick as a white elephant gift to Rebekah's holiday ornament party. She was such a character that everybody loved her and always asked if she was coming. She thought it would be funny to bring the brick she got from her grandson-in-law until she realized she had grown fond of that brick. So she went out and bought a different brick, wrapped it up, and brought it to the party.

Everybody drew a number and, when called, got to either steal someone's gift, or take a new gift from under the tree. When her number was called, my mother walked around the room, pretending to steal gifts and playfully grumbling at any person who stole a present from her. It was all in good humor.

A large man who looked like a threatening, leather-wearing, Harley motorcycle rider picked her brick from the pile of presents under the tree. After he opened the present, my mother squealed and playfully rebuked him for picking the brick she had gotten as a present from her grandson-in-law. He looked down at the brick peeking out from between his large hands and then apologetically looked back at my mother. When the party was over, he insisted on giving the brick back to her. She protested to no avail. Now she had two bricks.

In 2007, my mother turned 90 years old. Rebekah and I decided to plan a surprise birthday party for her. We rented a nice venue and invited everyone we knew, and those we didn't know, from her address book. People came from all over. Her best friend Edith's daughter came from Arkansas, and Amanda and her family showed up from Ohio. On the day of the party, Sam and I went to the clubhouse to get the guests ready to yell "Surprise," while Rebekah picked my mother up from her home. My mother thought the four of us were going to the clubhouse for dinner. She didn't seem to notice her friends' familiar cars in the parking lot.

Everybody yelled "SURPRISE!" as we entered the room. She threw her hands to her mouth as tears came to her eyes. I watched her as she floated around the room, laughing and socializing with her friends. At the age of 90 she still seemed so spry and agile. I stood up and gave a speech about her life that opened the opportunity for many people to stand up and say something about her. Here are a few excerpts from that speech:

"On April 8, 1917, my mother was born in a little log cabin with a dirt floor....

"My mother grew up to be a beautiful woman. She worked as an accountant's assistant and secretary to the Sergeant Major of an Army base. She was an independent, self-supporting young woman. Essentially, she was going about her business and enjoying her life. When she turned 30, her father sat her down and gave her a lecture about how she had better settle down and marry or she would end up a lonely old lady. She picked my father to settle down with, had two children, my brother and me, and remained married to him for 49 years, until he died at the age of 80....

"I asked my mother once what kind of man she thought would make an ideal husband. She thought for a moment and answered that he had to be someone who could support a wife and children and someone she could be happy with in a 50-50 relationship. She found that with my father. He worked and provided a living; she worked by staying home and raising the children. To her that was the way it was supposed to be....

"I asked her in what ways she thought life was different today. She answered that she thinks life is easier today because of all the new technology, but she misses the trust and respect people had for one another in earlier times. She commented that when a man made a deal with a handshake, he stood by his word....

"In my own personal experience, I can tell you that I was raised by a woman who also taught me to be independent. She thinks that even if a woman doesn't work outside the home, she can still maintain her independence. She taught me to be strong in times of hardship. She taught me self-respect. She taught me how to get through difficult times by using humor....

"Most of you know my mother to be spry and active. She still plays the organ for her church, she still bowls, and she exercises and goes for daily walks. I only hope I can follow in her footsteps. Happy birthday, Mom!"

Watching my mother in her element, flit around and visit with her friends, it would have been impossible to believe that five years later she wouldn't remember any of it.

In 2008, I broke three bones in my left leg while hiking in the mountains. I had to be rescued and taken to a hospital, where they performed surgery to place a titanium rod down the middle of my tibia, and bolts down my leg and in my ankle. I was unable to walk for many months.

My mother called and asked, "What are you doing?"

"Lying here with my leg up."

"What is Sam doing?"

"Cooking dinner."

"Poor Sam."

There I was, unable to walk without a walker or crutches and not able to put my leg down without pain and she showed no sympathy for me.

She remarked, "They should have put you in a nursing facility. How would you have liked that?"

Her statement gave me pause.

Occasionally, she drove over to visit me. My mother was known to drive her car fast. She was like the song, "Little Old Lady from Pasadena." She put her foot down on the gas pedal and slammed on her brakes when she needed to stop. Matt was following her in his car once when she slammed on the brakes and came screeching to a stop. He came to an abrupt stop behind her. When they got out of their respective cars, he told her she shouldn't slam on the brakes like that.

Her response was, "That's what the brakes are for."

In 2009, my mother fell again. This time she broke her wrist and bruised her hip. They kept her in the hospital for three days and then sent her to a nursing facility for three weeks to recover. She was incensed. She complained bitterly the whole time she was there. She didn't understand why she had to go there when she was perfectly capable of taking care of herself. I sympathized with her and visited her every night until she was able to go home. Again, she made a full recovery and was soon back to being her old spunky self.

Shortly after she got home, she called to tell me about a recent incident. She couldn't stop giggling as she told me about her adventure.

"When I got to the commissary to buy groceries, I parked the car in one of those handicap parking spots. After all, I have a permanent handicap license plate. I was in a hurry, so I started running."

Still giggling as she stumbled with her words, my mother continued, "As I ran toward the store, a man in the parking lot started yelling at me."

He noticed the disabled parking plates on her car and was agitated that she would take a disabled parking spot.

By this time, she was laughing so hard it was impossible to hear what she was saying.

"I stopped, turned around and looked at him, then yelled back, *'I'm an old lady!'* and then turned around and ran into the store."

On another occasion, my mother called me out of breath.

"Uh, Susan? I just had something terrible happen to me today."

She went on to say some man had called her and said she needed to write a cashier's check in the amount of $10,000 to cover an overdraft in her bank account. He said he would meet her at the bank's parking lot. She was convinced that he was telling the truth. Fortunately, she called her friend Ken and asked if he would go to the bank with her. Ken came over immediately and they went to the bank to see what was going on. Ken convinced her to go inside the bank first. The bank teller told them that she was so glad my mother had come to her first because she was being scammed. It was a scam that many older people fall for.

They all went outside to see if they could find the man, but there was nobody in the parking lot. I was grateful she had the presence of mind to call her friend Ken first. He calmed her down and they did the right thing. As my mother was very tight with her money, I wasn't surprised she didn't want to spend $10,000 unless she knew she had to.

Even though she had plenty of money in her banking account, my mother started complaining that she was getting late notices on her bills. She insisted she paid them in a timely manner and asked me to investigate it for her. I looked in her checkbook but couldn't find any entries that suggested she had paid. When I looked at her bank statements, I couldn't find any canceled checks indicating payment. I knew she had forgotten to pay the bills, so I suggested that I could easily pay her bills from her online account if she wanted me to do that for her. I was surprised when she agreed. She claimed her eyesight was getting worse and it was harder for her to write checks.

I knew she had macular degeneration in her left eye, but when I asked her about it, she said she could see fine and that she could still see great out of her one good eye.

By now I was starting to recognize my mother's deviant state of mind. I was relieved that I oversaw the paying of her bills. I went to her house to collect them, went home and paid them online. She was very appreciative and continued to blame her oversights with her bills on her failing eyesight. It also gave her an excuse to call me and ask me to come over immediately so she could give me her bills and ask me to check her bank statement. Paying her bills also gave me the chance to observe her more often. I noticed the papers piled on the kitchen table, which was unusual. Her bathroom floors started to look dirty, but I attributed it to the fact her eyesight was failing.

I started noticing her anxiety over events that had never made her nervous before. She invited the family, including Rebekah's husband's mother, to her house for her famous Christmas Eve chili and cornbread. Making chili was something she could do in her sleep and she loved having the family over. She asked me if I could help her set the table and serve it up in bowls. As we were cleaning up, I heard her breathe a deep sigh of relief. I had never seen her so nervous about fixing dinner before. I made a mental note that this was probably her last Christmas Eve of making chili for everyone.

As time went on, I started noticing my mother's strange behavior more often. One Thanksgiving, the family was in the living room of my house, laughing and talking. I left the room and when I returned, I noticed from the corner of my eye that my mother was starting to stand up from the couch. I crossed the room and just as I got to the center, there she stood, looking into my eyes, and standing in my way. She had calculated that move and I was impressed at her precision, but I wondered just how many times she had concocted other events like this. Was she trying to agitate me or get me to notice her? Putting my hands squarely on her shoulders, I told her to go sit down. She smirked but did as I asked. When I was cooking in the kitchen, she came in and tried to stand in the way again. Instead of letting it irritate me, I gave her a spoon and asked her to stir the gravy. This seemed to pacify her, and she stood by the stove and stirred the gravy as she had done so many times before.

My mother didn't often compliment me, nor did she show sentiment. So I was surprised when, that summer, she sent me a beautiful, heart-felt birthday card. I was moved because she usually sent me a generic card, signing it "Love and Prayers, Mom."

I called her to thank her for the card and tell her how much it meant to me.

"Hi, Mom. How have you been?" I asked.

"Oh, I'm fine. Happy birthday. By the way, that card I sent you was the only birthday card I could find in the whole store."

"Oh, okay. Well it was nice," I replied.

I was taken aback even though I should have known it was too much for her to express any kind of love or affection.

One late Friday night, my mother called to say she was having trouble with her eyes. I went over and saw they were very red and agitated. I told her we shouldn't wait until Monday to see the doctor but should immediately go to the emergency room. That wasn't what she wanted to hear; she wanted to wait to see her doctor on Monday. I insisted and got her in the car and took her to the emergency room. The triage nurse called her up to the desk almost immediately because of her age and then asked my mother her pain level from one to ten.

My mother exclaimed, "One!"

I sighed. This was going to be a long night as the triage nurses let in others before us. We waited hours before getting attention, and then we waited hours after they put us in a room. The tests revealed that she had an eye infection, and the doctor prescribed three types of medication to put in her eyes three times a day. I became aware that my mother couldn't understand the directions, even when I wrote them down step by step. I went over to her neighbor's house and asked if she would come and help my mother with her medication. She loved my mother and was willing to help.

I continued to visit my mother on Sundays. I sat in one of her overstuffed rocking chairs while she sat in the other and we hashed over past experiences, while Sam sat over on the loveseat and promptly fell asleep. She once brought up the conversation of my dream interpretations. She told me her mother interpreted dreams for other people as well. I found that interesting. I didn't know that about my grandmother. My mother asked me to interpret one of her dreams.

"I'm driving my car backwards down a hill and the car starts going faster and faster. I couldn't get the brakes to work," she recalled. "What do you think that means?" she asked.

I hesitated. I did not want to give her my true interpretation.

In a disgruntled tone she snorted, "You don't know anything!"

"You are going the wrong way in life very fast," I answered.

She seemed embarrassed and refused to discuss it further. She never mentioned any of her dreams again. I now ponder if the dream meant she was beginning to lose her mind and once she started down that slope, it was going to happen very quickly.

Realizing my mother's mind was failing, I wondered how long she would be able to live alone, much less drive a car. I had no idea just how difficult life was going to get as my mother's Alzheimer's disease progressed.

PART IV

A SLOW GOODBYE

"Uh, Susan?"

"Hi, Mom."

"Susan? Where am I? I'm in this here hotel or motel or whatever it is, and I don't know how I got here. When are you going to come get me and take me home?"

"Do you know how long you've been living there, Mom?"

"No, maybe a week?"

"You've been there for three months now. That is your home now."

"Really? I had no idea."

A few minutes go by and she asks, "Why, why am I here?"

I respond, "You can't live alone anymore. You have a hard time remembering things and you can't take care of yourself."

"Yes, I can. I can take care of myself. What do you mean?"

"Do you remember where you used to live? Can you tell me the address?"

"I can't remember. Where did I use to live?"

CHAPTER 19

Losing Her Memory

* * *

My mother was a strong, independent woman who lived alone in her house for 17 years before suddenly, in what seemed like one fell swoop, everything was taken away from her. All she really wanted was to laugh and enjoy her journey through life. A simple life that included going to her church, socializing with her friends, and spending time with her family. She loved to laugh, and her own laughter was contagious, sometimes beginning with what sounded like a hoot.

In her later years, though she feared falling and breaking her fragile bones, she'd insist on standing on ladders to change light bulbs, or chairs to reach the contents on a shelf in an upper cabinet. She did fall at least twice, resulting in first a broken hip, and then a broken wrist. But what was to cause her, to cause all of us, the most suffering, wasn't anything we feared in advance, no broken bones or bruises slow to heal. Instead, she slowly started losing her ability to function in her day-to-day life. She was taken to the hospital one day and never allowed to return to her home.

Helping my mother when she got Alzheimer's was one of the most difficult times in my life. I often felt guilty, frustrated, and depressed, but I also felt compassion and an unshakable sorrow. I cried at night, feeling an overwhelming sadness for her and at the same time, wishing she would die. I knew she would be horrified if she knew how she behaved at times. I also knew that if she were in her right state of mind, she would never have wanted to put this burden on me.

When she was afflicted with Alzheimer's, I could no longer call her and ask how her day was going. I could no longer laugh with her or commiserate or share an exciting moment with her. She could focus only on how she was feeling in the moment, and it was never going well. When I visited her, she sometimes sat with me and talked about long ago experiences. I wondered what it must be like for her, but I soon realized she wasn't logical, and I couldn't possibly know her thought process. I didn't realize how much I could miss my mother even while she was still alive. The last 13 months of her life were frustrating and stressful for both of us.

It was when my husband Sam and I lived in the San Francisco Bay Area that I started noticing shifts in my mother's behavior. She came to a party we were having and, as usual, wanted to help in the kitchen. I got the dessert ready to serve and decided to use an antique ceramic pie server that had once belonged to her mother. She had given it to me years earlier and it was beautiful and very special to me. While I was out of the room, Sam saw her deliberately throw it on the floor and unsuccessfully try to break it. He told me about it later and I was shocked. Why would she try to break it when she was the one who gave it to me in the first place? It didn't make sense at the time, but I shrugged it off, thinking maybe she was just angry at me for leaving her and going to the Bay Area to live.

During our phone conversations, I started noticing how she repeated her stories. A part of me wondered if she just wanted to keep the conversation going to prolong hanging up. Still, it nagged at me. When we moved back to Sacramento, I asked her doctor to test her for Alzheimer's. He refused, unless I broached it with her first and insisted that she take the test. I knew how furious she would be with me and knew how much it would devastate her if she lost her independence. Not confident enough to insist, I dropped it. At that time, I thought she was still competent enough to drive and live alone.

In 2010, I was diagnosed with breast cancer. Jim was also having difficulties with his health. We were both unable to function fully for about a year. I went through surgery, chemotherapy, and radiation, and during that time I was unable to give my mother the attention she needed or wanted. Sometimes when she called, I told Sam I was too sick to talk to her. She was shocked because I had never refused to talk to her before.

When I felt better, she wanted us to go shopping together. I suggested I come pick her up, but she insisted on driving herself over. I resigned myself because I knew when she made up her mind, there was no convincing her otherwise. When I got in her car, I noticed her driving was erratic. She seemed nervous and found it difficult to stay in her lane. She swerved into the next lane and then swerved back into her lane. I didn't want to dampen the mood, so I discreetly grabbed and hung on to the inside panel of the passenger door, saying nothing.

When we got to the store, we tried on clothes. She told me she wanted to buy me something. I found a cute shirt and when we got to the check-out counter, she sarcastically told the checker that she was the one who always had to drive me around. When she got out her wallet, she couldn't find any money, and because she had never owned a credit card, I paid for the clothes. I bit my tongue and didn't retaliate by telling the checker that I always had to buy her clothes, which, of course, wasn't true.

In the back of my mind, I was disturbed because my mother always had money in her wallet. She was very fastidious about how much money she got out of the bank each month to pay for groceries and other expenses. She always knew exactly how much she had and put money in different compartments in her purse for each type of expense. She even had a special place to put what she called her "whooping money," meaning money she could spend on something frivolous for herself.

Besides not having money in her purse, I started noticing other discrepancies in my mother's behavior. She called me one hot August evening to chat.

"Well, I just sent Jim and Doodle their birthday cards."

"Mom, their birthdays are in February; my birthday is in August."

Dead silence.

"Oh, shiiiiiit! I'm never going to live this down!"

That was the last time she tried to send anyone birthday cards.

About two months before my mother was diagnosed, she called me at work to tell me she had a "spell" when she tried to drive to the military commissary about two miles away from her home. I asked her what she meant by that.

She responded, "You know, a spell. Everybody has them. Don't you have those sometimes?"

"No, Mom, I don't. What kind of spell? How did you get home?"

"Oh, I just drove. I got home fine. But I don't think I will try driving there anymore."

And then she refused to say any more about it.

I called her one evening and she mentioned that she got lonely sometimes. I had never heard her say that before. My father had passed years ago, and she seemed to have a fulfilled life with her church and friends. She was always going somewhere, and we visited often as a family. I called her almost every night and visited on Sundays. I had never heard her complain of being lonely.

People with Alzheimer's often complain of being lonely, but I didn't make the connection. We talked about it for a while that night and the subject didn't come up again until after her diagnosis.

Some of the signs to pay attention to, if you suspect a loved one is getting Alzheimer's, are neglect of the home, such as a filthy bathroom, or the refrigerator, or the pantry having no food. Other signs are losing weight, an inability to manage bills, and not remembering to take medication. I noticed most of these signs long before she was diagnosed, even though I didn't know to look for them at the time.

My mother's church often had covered-dish dinners. I remember my mother telling me she made a chicken casserole for one of those dinners and that she put lima beans in it. I never remembered her adding lima beans before; it sounded awful. I asked her for the recipe. She couldn't remember how to make it even though she made it so often she didn't need a recipe. I thought that was strange and laughed when she told me her friends at her church requested that she make her famous carrot cake (from a box) in the future.

When I had a small gathering for dinner, she wanted to know what to bring to my house, so I asked her to make her signature deviled eggs. I thought that would be easy for her. Jim had picked her up; when she got to my house, I looked down and saw soggy eggs sitting in putrid-looking water. I knew we wouldn't be able to politely eat them, even if it meant hurting her feelings.

"Mom, did you put water in these eggs?" I asked.

She looked down and noticed the water sloshing around her eggs and became embarrassed.

"No! I made them the way I always make them."

She rushed by me, heading straight for the kitchen, and threw them in the trash. I followed her to make sure she knew where the trash was.

She turned around and grabbed me by the hands, whispering, "Please don't tell anybody, I'm so embarrassed. It must be my failing eyes."

While we sat around the table eating and enjoying good conversation, she was very quiet. I looked at her, noticing the nice scarf around her neck and just how well-dressed and put together she always looked. She refused a glass of wine as I served everyone, but then at one point she grabbed my wine and gulped it down. Her eyes became wide as she sputtered and choked.

"Mom, would you like some wine? I can give you your own glass."

She put my wine down, answering, "No, I'm fine."

Because of the macular degeneration in my mother's left eye, every year or so she was required to take a driving road test before renewing her driver's license. Before she was scheduled to take her test, Jim and I talked about what might happen if she lost her license. We both knew she wouldn't likely pass the test and wanted to prepare ourselves. We talked about her living in the country, and how we would have to help her if she lost her independence. We decided to take turns visiting her each week and planned out how we could make it work. I thought a part of her would be pleased because she would be guaranteed to see and spend time with each of us on a regular basis. I was in for a surprise.

My mother decided to take her driving test in March 2012 rather than wait until her birthday in April, in case she didn't pass the first time. She must have known it wasn't going to end well. As the time neared for her to take her test, I could feel her anxiety growing. She'd taken these tests for years and had never acted nervous before. This time was different. I think she knew she was losing her memory but was very good at disguising, at least from me, what was happening to her. I took the day off work, thinking that after she passed the driving test, we would go to lunch and celebrate, but deep down I knew she shouldn't be driving anymore.

I drove to her house to pick her up. She was almost ready, so I sat in one of the overstuffed rocking chairs that she loved. I looked at the little table between the chairs and noticed small pieces of paper with notes in her handwriting, detailing partial conversations that she'd had. It was obvious she was forgetting what people were saying to her and she was writing notes to remind herself what the conversation was about. I felt a deep sadness and knew then with certainty that her memory was failing. I looked up to see her ready to go. She gave me the keys to her car and asked if I would drive.

When we got to the Department of Motor Vehicles, I parked the car, and we went inside to tell them we had an appointment. She wanted to drive to the testing area herself, so she got in the driver's seat and I got in the passenger's seat. As she turned on the engine and started backing out, I looked in the passenger mirror and noticed a truck right behind us.

"Mom, STOP! STOP! STOP!"

I held my breath and grabbed the handle hold on the door. It took a few moments before her reflexes kicked in, but she finally jolted to a halt. She took a deep breath and waited until a man helped her back the car out safely. I noticed that it was difficult for her to follow his directions. As she pulled the car forward, another car was coming toward us. Again, I clutched my seat and gritted my teeth, as she came so close that she missed the other car by mere inches. I started to say something but bit my tongue when I saw the intense look on her face. She slowly rolled around the parking lot until she was in front of the long, narrow testing entrance and inched her way in. There was a car directly in front of her, but she seemed not to notice until the last moment, when she jolted to a stop. I let out the breath that I had been holding in, and made a mental note that we had almost had three accidents in the parking lot! We got out of the car and sat on a cement bench in the waiting section until the tester came to get her. She was breathing heavily and rubbing her hands together anxiously.

"I'm so nervous about this."

Putting my arms around her I tried to console her.

"You're going to be fine. You've passed this driving test many times before with no problem."

She nodded her head but was still fidgeting.

"Okay, Mom, take a deep breath and then let it out."

She took several deep breaths and tried to gather herself together.

The tester told her to get into the driver's seat as he got into the passenger's seat next to her. He looked bored, no doubt thinking it was another routine driving test. I chuckled to myself; he had no idea what he was in for. He took a quick look at me and said they would be back in about 20 minutes. Ten minutes later, they were back. I could tell by the look on the tester's face it hadn't gone well. The bored look he had earlier was replaced with an apprehensive, wild-eyed, get-me-the-hell-out-of-this-car look.

He unsteadily got out of the car, saw me, and asked, "Are you her daughter?" I nodded in acknowledgment.

Taking me aside he said, "I'm revoking her license. Will you warn her for me so that it doesn't come as a surprise?"

I was relieved, knowing that it was the right decision, and that I didn't have to make it. We sauntered back inside as the tester left us alone, giving me an opportunity to warn her about what was coming.

"Mom, they are going to revoke your license."

She looked quietly down at her hands.

I continued, "Don't worry. Jim and I will help you and make sure you are able to go shopping and run errands." I thought I was making progress. The tester watched from a distance and waited for a while before coming over.

"I'm revoking your license," the tester said with authority.

My mother looked up at him in disbelief.

"Is this permanent or can I take the test again?"

"It's permanent. We're revoking your license."

My mother had always been self-composed. I had seen her in many situations and never saw her lose her temper in public. If anything, she had a quiet, stoic way of letting you know she wasn't happy. And you always knew when she wasn't happy.

She started yelling at the top of her lungs, "I LIVE IN THE COUNTRY! HOW AM I GOING TO BE ABLE TO GO SHOPPING FOR GROCERIES? HOW AM I GOING TO BE ABLE TO TAKE CARE OF MYSELF?"

The tester started backing away as I looked around the room at all the people staring at us. I looked down and silently told myself I'd probably never see these people again.

Discretely, I took my mother's hand and said, "Let's get out of here."

As I drove her home, I reiterated, "You're not alone. Jim and I will be here to help you."

She wasn't listening to me.

Muttering to herself she said, "I couldn't help running into the curb, there was a bump in the street. There was a reason I couldn't stay in my lane. It wasn't that bad. It was just a little bump."

I could only imagine what that tester had gone through after the near-miss accidents I had gone through myself with her in the parking lot.

She insisted, "If I could just take the test again, I could pass it. Is there any way I can take the test again?"

I let her vent, sympathized with her, and was grateful that I wasn't the one who had taken her driver's license away. When we got to her house, we went inside, and I decided to spend the rest of the day with her.

I looked over at her and asked, "How're you doing?"

"I am so depressed. This is worse than losing your father."

"Well, you've been driving longer." I was trying to make her laugh. It worked for a moment.

We went out to one of her regular places for dinner, but she refused to eat, saying, "I'm not hungry."

When we got back to the house it was getting late, and I asked, "Are you going to be okay?"

"Yes, I'm fine. You can go home."

The next day was Saturday and I was going to spend the day with her again when I got a call from the husband of one of my best friends. My friend had died that morning after battling cancer for 10 years. I made the decision to go to his house instead.

On Sunday, my mother got a ride to church and spent the rest of the day with her friends. Jim said he was going to come down and spend Thursday with her, so I thought that would be a good time for us to sit her down and talk to her in person. I called her throughout the week to see how she was doing. Her voice was hoarse, and she had a cough. She said she was coming down with a cold. Other than that, she seemed to be in good spirits. I repeated how Jim and I would take turns each week and help her and that if she needed anything I would be there as soon as I could. I thought she was coming to terms with her situation and that in time, once we started a regular routine, she would be fine.

On Thursday Jim called me at work from her house.

"Mom seems to be getting sicker. Do you think we should take her to the hospital?"

"Yes, probably. I'll stop and get a pizza so we can eat it there. I'll be there as soon as I can."

When I got to her house, Jim told me she had just passed out. He said he had been making her get ready to go to the emergency room but that she was resisting. She hadn't wanted to go, insisting on going to her bedroom to change her clothes and brush her teeth. As he waited, he heard a thump and went back to her bedroom to find her passed out. She had hit the dresser as she went down, but recovered quickly, and he helped her back to the living room. I found her sitting in her chair with her hands folded in her lap and looking grim.

I asked, "How are you feeling?"

"I'm fine."

I got us each a piece of pizza and as we ate, I said, "You need to go to the hospital to make sure everything is all right."

Through clenched teeth she spat, "I'm fine!"

"Well, you don't have a choice. We are taking you to the hospital."

"I need to change my clothes and brush my teeth first."

She got out of the chair and started down the hall with me right behind her. She jumped when she noticed me behind her and let out a loud sigh to let me know she wasn't happy about any of this. She was using every tactic possible to delay going. When she was finally through brushing her teeth, changing her clothes, and brushing her hair, we went back to the living room where Jim patiently waited for us.

The evening was getting gloomy and cold, so we stopped by the front door closet to get her a coat. She resisted our help as we struggled to get her coat on her. The effort took most of her energy and I barely caught her, just as she passed out again.

Jim picked up her feet, "Okay, let's get her to the car."

He opened the front door and backed out while I struggled to hold on to her.

Breathlessly I muttered, "Wait, I'm going to drop her. I need to catch my breath. She is really heavy!"

Jim managed to open the rear car door, and with a final shove, we laid her down in the back seat. I drove to the emergency room, where they immediately took her in. On the way to the hospital, Jim and I again discussed her declining cognitive abilities and how we would take turns helping her. He would come down alternating Thursdays and help her shop or do whatever she needed, and I would take over on the other Thursdays. She was still unconscious when we arrived.

My mother would most likely have died that night if Jim hadn't been there. In retrospect, she probably should have.

CHAPTER 20

In the Hospital Before Diagnosis

"This is Nadine, Susan. I'm trying to get through to you right now. I've been calling [my phone number] and if I have you, would you please give Mom a call?"

***

When my mother woke up in the emergency room, she was disoriented and scared, lying on a bed with the curtains closed around her. I sat in a small chair beside her. A doctor finally came by to give us the results of the tests, which determined she had pneumonia and a urinary tract infection. He mentioned her advance health directive, which the hospital had on file, that instructed the doctors not to give her life-support treatments. If she hadn't been paying attention before, she was now. Her eyes flew open, her mouth gaped, and she tried to sputter something incoherently.

I looked at the doctor and said, "We don't need to comply with the directive at this time."

She closed her eyes briefly, then looked up at me with relief.

It seemed an eternity before she was checked into a room at the hospital. Sam and I stayed with her until she had settled down for the night, and then we went home and fell into bed. I tossed and turned before finally dozing into a fitful sleep. I felt numb. I took deep breaths and told myself everything was going to be fine, but I knew something dreadful was unfolding.

The next morning, when I entered her room, I noticed she was tied to the bed. She looked up at me and tried to move her arms, but the soft straps kept her secured.

In a small whimpering voice, she sobbed, "This is so unnecessary."

The nurse came in and apologetically said she kept getting up and they hadn't been able to keep her in her bed the night before. It was hospital procedure to tie a patient down if they couldn't comply.

"Mom, why did you keep getting out of bed?" I asked.

She cried out, "They wouldn't let me go to my own party! They were throwing a party for me, there must have been a hundred people, and they wouldn't let me go. It was MY party!"

She repeated this same version over and over; she was hallucinating. I knew something was drastically wrong. A feeling of dread crept into my stomach, and in that moment, life as I knew it, would be changed forever. My mother was upset and wanted to go home. She asked me several times where her purse was.

"I took your purse home with me because we both thought it would be safer. I'll bring it back tomorrow."

I had also slipped her big diamond rings off her fingers and took them home with me. She asked, "Susan, where are my rings?"

"I took them home and I'm going to put them in my safe deposit box at the bank until you get to go home."

She was satisfied. "That's a good idea. Thank you."

After Sam and I got home late that night, I went to bed exhausted but still unable to sleep. I felt a buzz throughout my body, but eventually fell into a restless doze.

The next morning, I got my mother's purse and took every kind of identification out of it, including the checks out of her checkbook. I worried that she was going to notice and rebuke me, but she never looked inside her purse. I placed it next to her in her bed and she slept with that purse by her side for the remainder of her stay in the hospital. It gave her comfort; it was her identity.

She knew something was happening to her. She sat up in bed and rocked back and forth, holding her head and crying that something was happening inside her head.

I put my arms around her and tried to comfort her. "I'm right here. We'll get through this together."

I held back tears, feeling helpless and inadequate.

The doctor took me aside to speak in private. She thought my mother had sundowners syndrome and said my mother would never be able to live by herself again. I had never heard of sundowners before. I found out that sundowners syndrome affects people with dementia and Alzheimer's disease. It causes agitation, fear, an uncontrolled sadness, and basic mood and behavior changes that get worse when the sun goes down. Eventually, those affected lose their language skills and abstract thought.

After a couple of weeks in the hospital, we arranged to put her in a nursing home. I chose the one she had been in before when she broke her hip. I remembered she liked the physical therapy services there.

CHAPTER 21

After Diagnosis

"Susan? This is Nadine. I'm down here at this here hotel or motel or whatever it is. I've forgotten. You know which one it is, I think. Anyway, my number is [my phone number] in case you've forgotten what number to call. Give me a call, would you please?"

* * *

While my mother was in the nursing home, I visited her every day and stayed for as long as I could tolerate it. It was difficult listening to her constant complaints, and demands that I get her out of that place. I settled on visiting her right after work, before dinner, so I could go home and have dinner with Sam. I helped her get ready for bed, turned on the television, and left her with a program she liked.

Once, I was at my desk at work when I received a call from a friend who liked to play pranks on me. I usually recognized his voice, but my mind was in other places. He told me he was from the nursing facility and was very sorry, but my mother had taken a taxi and left. I panicked. I could imagine my mother doing just that! He finally started laughing. I started breathing again, letting out a long sigh of relief, and rebuked him for scaring in this way.

Then one afternoon the nurses helped my mother call me at work.

"Susan! They set me free!"

"What do you mean, they set you free?"

She excitedly exclaimed, "Susan? They set me free! I'm running free down the halls!"

She wasn't making sense.

"Mom, where is your room? You need to go back to your room."

"I don't know where my room is."

Without a moment's hesitation I asked, "Where is your purse?"

"My purse? It is in my room."

"Okay Mom, you need to go sit by your purse."

"Oh, okay, I will do that."

Since she kept her purse beside her for some sort of comfort, this was an effective way to calm her down, though she still hadn't noticed that most of the content was empty. As time passed, I got more and more of these calls from her, and I had to devise more and more innovative ways to respond. It was stressful trying to figure out how to deal with my mother. I knew nothing about Alzheimer's or how to deal with it, learning painfully as I went.

My mother continually demanded, "Get me out of this place!"

I tried reasoning with her, telling her the place she was in was only temporary, but I couldn't cogently connect with her. She was filled with anxiety and there was no calming her down. She even became obsessed with her roommate in the bed next to her, and wouldn't leave the poor woman alone. She constantly went over, bent down close, and peered into her roommate's face to see if she was all right. At various hours of the night my mother got up and woke her to see if she needed anything. This behavior was so unlike my mother, who normally would have kept to herself.

After a few weeks, the doctor at the nursing home decided to send her home, but Sam asked him to take a closer look. The doctor asked her questions and gave her tests, such as drawing a clock or naming items in a room, to help determine cognitive decline.

The doctor asked, "Who is today's president?"

She looked up at him and said, "Hoover."

She noticed we gave her a strange look, so she looked sweetly at the doctor and coyishly disguised her answer as a joke. I wondered if she was flirting with the doctor, but realized she was trying to divert our attention. My mother was excellent at camouflaging her real state of mind. When she was unable to answer simple questions, it soon became evident she couldn't remember anything from the present. I was shocked when I learned she couldn't remember her address, especially since she had lived in her house over 25 years. She couldn't remember her neighborhood or the city she lived in. After the assessment we were certain that she could never go home and live alone.

The caretakers at the nursing home asked Sam and me for a private consultation. When they got us alone, they suggested we put my mother in a home. I looked online and found a person that specialized in finding places for seniors who have conditions like my mother's. I discovered that these professionals usually consult for free, and if one of their recommended facilities is chosen, the facility pays them a commission. After the consultant came to the nursing home and assessed her, Jim and I began the process of finding my mother an appropriate place to live. Much later, unfortunately, we realized that the consultant gave us names of large institutions that wouldn't work in our case. Not only did they cost more than a smaller home, but they were too large for someone like my mother.

A woman from my mother's church who took care of seniors asked my mother and me if my mother could live with her. My mother started giggling with excitement. As we headed into her small bathroom so she could brush her teeth and get ready for bed, she was giddy and couldn't keep still. The next day, the woman called me and said her husband wouldn't let my mother move in. He was worried she might become physically aggressive, as some Alzheimer's patients do, and they weren't equipped to handle that. As the woman apologized, I started thinking of a way to break the news to my mother. When I visited her, she didn't remember the invitation from the day before, and I didn't mention it.

I looked at her finances and crunched the numbers, deciding she could afford a nice place for about 10 years. Considering she was already 95, if she were still alive when her funds ran out, I could then place her in a less expensive establishment, and it wouldn't likely make a difference to her.

After looking at all the places on the list, Jim and I finally found a facility where there was a beautiful one-bedroom apartment with a small living area, kitchen, bathroom, and a balcony. We fell in love with it. I could picture her standing on her balcony looking out at the trees or sitting at a little table, sipping on a cup of coffee. We looked at each other and decided we would love to live here if something like this happened to us. We thought she would grow to love it.

Meanwhile, back at the nursing facility, she was still complaining loudly and demanding bitterly that I get her out of that place. I told her I was working on it, and that we had found her a nice place to live.

"What do you mean, a nice place to live? I want to go home."

"Mom, the doctor isn't going to let you go home and live alone. If you want, we can get somebody to live with you."

"No, I don't want anybody to come live with me. Why can't I go home?"

"I think you will like this new place. They will help you manage your medicine, give you baths, and take you to a nice dining area to eat. It is also very close to me so I can come visit often."

"It's close to you?"

"Yes, I will be close by if you need anything."

"Why can't I come live with you?"

"I'm not at home during the day. I have to go to work."

"But I could help clean the house and have dinner ready when you get home."

"I'm only five minutes away and you can come and spend the night sometimes."

This was too much for me to take in. I didn't want her to live with me, but my heart went out to her. She was too anxious and restless, and I knew it would not only be unfair to me, but also to Sam. Later, when I knew more about Alzheimer's, I wondered how she would have reacted if we had told her we were taking her home. Would she have known the difference? Then there were times when I felt guilty and wondered if I could have managed having her live with me. What I didn't know then, but now know, is that taking care of a person with Alzheimer's is a 24-hour, seven-days-a-week job. We would never have been able to leave her alone.

I hired movers and we took a little love seat, one of the two recliner chairs she loved to sit in, her china cabinet, end tables, and her hard rock maple bedroom furniture to the new facility. I also took over a few items for the kitchen. We dolled the place up to look as much like her home as possible. Even though I knew she would never be able to live alone again, I didn't know what to do with her house.

When I went over to her house, some of her neighbors came to greet me. One of them said to me that my mother needed to be in a home. The other one said she had started feeding my mother meals because she wasn't able to fend for herself anymore. Other friends of hers took her out for lunch almost every day. I had no idea this was going on and realized just how far her mind had already declined.

Because her house was 30 to 45 minutes away from me, I worried about leaving it empty, so a few months after we moved her into the care facility, Jim and I decided to put it up for sale. I didn't have the energy to take care of her house, my house, and her too. It sold within a few weeks.

The assisted living facility Jim and I picked out gave her a room on the third floor, at the far end of the hall. Considering she was in good shape, I thought it would be good exercise for her to walk down the hall, to and from the elevator. I didn't realize how difficult it was going to be for her just to remember how to get to the elevator.

Jim and I took her from the nursing home to the new apartment we were so proud to have found. It was beautiful inside and out, and very clean. The dining room was on the first floor and we showed her around the place, waiting for her to respond.

She looked at me with her steely blue eyes and said with disgust, "I would never have picked this place for myself. This is way too fancy."

I knew she was frightened and tried to reason with her.

"Mom, remember that time I wanted to show you places to live in case the day came for you to move? You said you weren't ready and refused to go look."

She briskly replied, "I'm still not ready."

I sighed, "But now we have no choice. This is the place Jim and I picked out for you. If you don't like it, we can find another place. You don't have to stay here."

We took her up to her apartment and tried to settle her in. At one point I took her to the bathroom, where she complained that there was no bathtub. I knew she always took baths, but this place had a large shower instead. Later, on one of my visits, she told me she could get enough water in the bottom of the shower to sit and take a bath. I laughed.

She perched herself on a chair, looking dignified, while her children tried to appease her. She was content for a while, having Jim, Rebekah, Sam, and me around her, and then Jim and Rebekah left, and Sam and I remained. She started to panic when I stood up, and I wondered if I was ever going to be able to leave, when I heard a knock on the door. One of the caretakers came by to greet her and help make her feel more comfortable. The caretaker playfully teased her, telling her she could have sleepovers and would have so much fun living there. I finally left, feeling exhausted. I called her when I got home, and she seemed to have settled down.

I still had no idea what was in store for us.

Although we had moved some of her furniture over so it would feel familiar, the place was tiny. The stove had been permanently turned off and I was amazed she never figured that out. We also bought her a smaller microwave so she could heat water for her instant coffee—something she had loved to fix for us when we came to visit in the past. She said she was having trouble seeing the buttons to push on the microwave, so Sam put some of her corn pads over certain buttons and told her which ones to push. Once, when we first went to visit her, we kept hearing a beeping sound coming from the kitchen. I discovered the beep was from the microwave, and looked inside to find that the water for the coffee was cold. No telling how long that microwave had been beeping, but she seemed not to notice.

I set up an appointment with her doctor, whom she dearly loved. I told her to be ready by 10:00 that morning. I arrived early and found her in her nightgown. I was confused and asked if she would rather not go see him, but that wasn't the problem. She just hadn't remembered to get dressed. I went with her to her bedroom and picked out an outfit. She started anxiously resisting until slowly I got her dressed.

"How do I look?" she asked.

My mother was always well put together. Her clothes were stylish, and I had found a cute outfit for her to wear.

"You look great!" I replied.

She kept fidgeting and resisting until I began to think we weren't going to make it on time. I squirted her with a little perfume and hustled her out the door.

As he greeted us, her doctor looked concerned. It was obvious that this wasn't the same woman he was used to seeing. He took her off most of the medication the nursing facility had put her on, and when we tried to set up another appointment, he refused to see her again. I'm not sure why, but I wondered if it was because he realized she was losing her mind and did not want to be responsible for her care anymore.

When we returned to her apartment building, she got confused and went down the hall, looking at each apartment number and trying to remember which one was hers. I put a sign that said "Nadine" on the outside of the door, but she either never remembered to look for it, or else didn't recognize her name. The caretakers escorted her back and forth to her room each time she went downstairs for a meal. Sometimes I found her frantically roaming the halls on the first floor. She didn't know how to get on the elevator to get back to her room, and couldn't find her room even when she was on the right floor. It was excruciating to watch.

On a piece of paper, I wrote, in large print, my phone number and the phone numbers of some of her close friends and family. She went down that list, and called each number 20 to 50 times a day. It was frustrating and depressing. I couldn't possibly answer the phone every time she called, so most times I didn't answer. When I couldn't stand it any longer, I answered, and heard her whimpering and pleading voice. I felt the guilt and shame of not being there for her in her time of desperate need. Sometimes I could calm her down by telling her I was just five minutes away. Sometimes she lashed out and accused me of putting her "in this place." After hanging up the phone, she often called back within five minutes, and didn't remember the conversation we had just had.

Every time I visited my mother, there was clutter all about. She constantly moved things around and made a mess. I helped her pick the place up and put it back together again, remembering how immaculate my mother had always kept her home. One time I found checks and important papers strewn all about. Confused, I finally realized they'd been stored in the little antique liquor cabinet we'd brought from her house. It hadn't occurred to me to look inside before taking it over to her new place. I knew this wasn't like her and at times I became frustrated, remembering how cute and quaint her new place once looked.

Jim called her one day to chat. He wrote down the conversation he had with her.

"Everything is thrown loose. Nothing is left to waste, they use everything. That's crazy. I can't live here any longer. It all gets around."

The conversation didn't make sense.

Once when I went to visit, I noticed that all the family pictures I had placed around her apartment were turned over.

"Mom? Why have you turned the pictures facedown?"

Bleakly she answered, "I didn't want to see their smiling faces."

It occurred to me that she didn't even know who they were. It saddened me because I knew she was miserable and there was nothing I could do—there was nothing she could do.

One evening around 8:00 my mother called me and asked, "Who is this?"

I responded, "This is Susan."

"Susan? Are you coming over?"

"I'm coming over tomorrow night, Mom. I usually visit you Mondays and Thursdays."

"We need to get together and talk. Do I have to live here? Can you come over tonight so we can talk about it?"

"You don't have to live there if you don't want to. We can go visit other places. Can it wait until tomorrow night? It's getting late."

"I really want you to come over now. We need to talk about all this."

This went on until she wore me down.

"Okay, we'll be over in about 10 minutes."

When Sam and I got to her apartment, she was looking smug and contrite. I brought up the subject of her moving.

She said, "I just wanted you to come over. I don't know why, but it makes me feel good to be able to make you come over."

I sighed, "Well, now that we're here, why don't we go ahead and talk about where you want to live?"

"No, I don't want to talk about it now. I just wanted you to come over."

I realized she was cognizant enough to plan an event and follow through. She knew she wanted me to visit her and she used her manipulation skills to make it happen. Maybe she wasn't as bad as we thought. Maybe she would be able to go home and live someday. Maybe I had made a mistake in moving her to a permanent place where she clearly wasn't comfortable.

I asked her if she could remember the address where she used to live. She was unable to tell me. She said she wanted to go home but she couldn't remember her home. I pondered what would happen if she went back to her old house. How would she do? I could have made it happen earlier, even though it wasn't close to where I lived, and I wouldn't have been able to go over to her house quickly or easily. It also would have been very expensive to hire someone to help take care of her there. Would her friends have helped? These were questions that haunted me.

She told me she missed her church, so I agreed to take her to church on Sundays and said her friend could bring her home. I made the arrangement with her friend, thinking I had found a solution that she would enjoy.

The first Sunday I took her to church we drove down the street near her neighborhood, the same street she had driven a million times when she lived there. I anxiously waited for her to ask me to drive by her house, but she just sat in the car fiddling with her hands. She never mentioned her home. I pulled up to the church parking lot and saw one of the members. I took her over to him, asked if he would help her, and told him her friend was going to take her home. He agreed and I left.

After church they took her out to dinner as they usually did, and then returned her to her new home. Her friend called me and said my mother had acted very nervous and didn't seem to enjoy herself.

The next Sunday I asked my mother if she was ready to go to church but she refused to go. I didn't understand that she wasn't remembering her church, her friends, or even her home. I called her several more Sundays to see if she was ready, but she never went back. I couldn't get a clear answer from her as to why she didn't want to go. I finally understood that she had lost complete memory of her home and church.

She remembered her close friends for a while, especially if they told her who they were. She had their phone numbers from the list I had prepared for her and called them many times during the day. I finally deleted their phone numbers when they started complaining. She didn't seem to notice the missing phone numbers and never mentioned them again. I noticed that when she called me, she always told me to return her call and would give my phone number instead of hers. Because I didn't write down her phone number, she didn't remember it and would read my number off the paper I gave her.

One night my mother called.

"Uh, Susan?"

"Hi, Mom."

"Where am I? I'm in this here hotel or motel and I'm waiting for someone to come pick me up and take me home."

"We could do that, but you would need somebody to live with you. You can't live alone anymore. Can you think of somebody you could live with or do you want me to hire somebody to live with you?"

"No, I don't want that. Why can't I live by myself?"

"Well, you need somebody to cook your meals and give you your medicine."

"I don't want to live here. Do I have to live here?"

"No, Mom. We can go and look at other places. You don't have to live there if you don't like it there."

"Well, I do like it here. This place is really nice, and the people are so nice to me. Maybe we should think about this."

"Okay, we can always go look at other places whenever you want."

We repeated this same conversation several times and then hung up. I visited her several times a week until her mind started declining even further and eventually cut it back to once a week—usually Thursdays. Every time I went to visit, she thought it was Sunday.

Sometimes she would have a lucid moment and ask me about her finances.

"Susan? What has happened to my house?"

"Nothing, Mom, it is still there." I didn't think it was necessary to stress her with the truth.

"Where is all my furniture? Is it still there?"

Even though some of it was in her new apartment, I answered, "Yes."

"Well, tell me this. Who is paying for all of this?"

"The VA is paying for all of this. We are so lucky, aren't we?"

I didn't want her to know she was paying for it, from her savings and the proceeds from her house, so I lied.

"Yes, we are so lucky. Dad really did right by us, didn't he?"

Fortunately, she believed me. I told her I was taking care of her bills because she had granted me power of attorney to manage her affairs. I was waiting for the day when she would accuse me of stealing her money, as I heard often happens with those who suffer with Alzheimer's, but that day never came. She trusted me completely.

I encouraged her to go downstairs and join one of the many activities the home provided, but she refused to go unless I took her. Once, when I took her downstairs there was a group of women sitting around chatting. I introduced my mother to them. They greeted her and shared where they had been raised. Then they started repeating the same conversation. As one woman started to repeat her story, I reiterated a part of her story. She looked surprised and asked, "How did you know?"

I didn't get a chance to respond before she apologized and said, "I might repeat the same story over and over."

My mother laughed and replied, "That's okay, I'll forget it anyway."

As they laughed, I was amused that they were able to jest about themselves despite this horrific condition.

As we sat around in the cool, beautiful lounge on a sweltering summer day, one woman started a discussion, saying, "The squirrels aren't out today."

The next person said, "They are usually scrambling from tree to tree."

My mother added, "That is what they do."

I said, "Well, it is very hot out there today."

Then the first person started over with, "The squirrels aren't out today."

The next person added, "They are usually scrambling from tree to tree."

My mother: "That is what they do."

It was now my turn again, so I kept it going by repeating, "Well, it is very hot out there today."

And this went on for several more rounds; each time I repeated my line when it was my turn.

When I visited, I usually took her downstairs, hoping she would eventually make friends. There were many activities, bingo being one of them. She loved playing bingo but still wouldn't go downstairs unless I took her. Sometimes the staff took her, but she never went on her own.

Sam often went with me when I visited her. I tried to keep a positive attitude and was almost successful until the minute I stepped inside the building and was hit with a sweet, sickening smell and the soft sound of music. Arriving at my mother's apartment, I knocked and then went in. She never locked the door, but I had a key if I'd needed it. Once when Sam was right behind me, she suddenly opened the door. She stood there completely naked.

I slammed the door closed and looked at Sam, saying, "You don't need to see this."

Sam replied, "Too late."

I went inside. "Mom, what are you doing? It is 2:00 in the afternoon. You should be dressed!"

She was fidgeting around and had a vacant look in her eyes. She didn't know who or where she was. I wanted to scream. Never in a million years would my mother ever have wanted to live like this. I took her to her bedroom and helped her dress. By the time I let Sam in, she was more coherent. I worried that she would start running down the halls naked as I had heard some do. I knew if that happened, we would have to move her into lockdown—a place where they keep Alzheimer's patients so they cannot get out and get lost. That was the only time she answered the door naked.

When we visited on Thursdays, we usually took her out for coffee or frozen yogurt, depending on the weather. As soon as she got in the car she asked, "Is this Sunday?"

"No, Mom, this is Thursday."

"Oh, that's right. I don't know why I thought it was Sunday."

I realized that in the past I had mostly visited her on Sundays and that was the confusion.

Now when I visited, I started going through her apartment, taking home her jewelry or anything else that seemed important. There was no reason to take a chance that she would throw away something valuable or misplace it. If she were in the apartment, she would get anxious and tell me not to take anything away, not even her larger clothes, which she didn't need or wear anymore because she had lost a lot of weight. I knew she would never miss any of it, if I could just get them out when she wasn't there. If we knew she was already downstairs, Sam would find her while I went up to her apartment to sneak out her valuables. Then I would bring the car around to the front to pick Sam and her up.

One time, I wondered why Sam was taking so long. He told me later that when he went up to her, he took her elbow and said, "We're here to take you out for coffee, Nadine." She became very nervous and agitated, and he realized she didn't recognize him.

He said, "Nadine, it's me. Sam."

"Oh, Sam. How are you?"

She remembered him as soon as he said his name.

"We are taking you for coffee."

"Oh, how nice. I would love to go have coffee with you."

They finally came out, with her clutching Sam's arm.

Another time when I went to visit by myself, I was delighted to see her sitting outside in conversation with another woman, and hopeful she was making friends. It felt good to see her sitting outside enjoying herself. I went up and sat with them.

After a while I asked, "Do you want to go for coffee?"

The woman next to her got up to leave and remarked, "I would love to go have coffee with my daughter."

Without hesitation my mother commented, "But that isn't my daughter."

I was shocked. That was the first time she didn't recognize me. I was not prepared for the feelings that overcame me, even though, logically, I knew this happened with those who had Alzheimer's. My eyes teared and I wanted to yell at her, "I am your daughter!"

Even though my mother called me every day—many, many times—I occasionally was able to call her.

"Hi, Mom."

"Who is this?"

"This is your daughter, Susan."

"Oh, Susan. How nice to hear from you. Susan? I don't know where I am. Can you tell me where I am?"

Sigh. *Take a deep breath*, I thought, *she can't help herself*. She was getting worse.

"Mom, I'm coming over to take you out to dinner."

"Oh, that would be great. I would love that."

"I'm on my way. I'll be there in five minutes."

"Okay, I'll be ready."

But when I got there, she wasn't ready. Other times, she wasn't in her apartment and I had to look for her. Sometimes the caretakers had taken her downstairs for dinner or to play games, or I'd often find my mother wandering the halls.

I'd say, "Let's go get a cup of coffee."

"Okay, that would be great."

"Sam is outside waiting for us in the car."

Inside the car my mother would ask, "What day is it today? Is it Sunday?"

"No, Mom. Today is Thursday."

"Oh, I just don't know why I can't remember what day it is."

One chilly night we took her out for hot chocolate. While sitting at the coffee shop, trying to enjoy ourselves, my mother's finger started to spasm at the joint. The finger took a 90-degree turn to the side. It looked like it was broken, and I became concerned as I watched.

My mother said, "I hate it when it does that."

I asked, "Does it hurt?"

"No."

That was it. I stopped looking at it.

She called me one Saturday morning while I was babysitting my grandsons. Even though she was the one who called, my mother asked, "Who is this?"

"This is Susan, who is this?"

"This is Nadine, your mom. What are you doing?"

"I'm babysitting. We are outside going for a walk to the park."

"Are you coming over?"

"Not for a while, I'm babysitting."

"Well, I need for you to come over! When are you coming over?"

"I'll be over later. Right now, I'm babysitting."

"WELL, WHAT ABOUT ME? WHAT ABOUT ME?" she screamed.

"I'll be over soon. When I'm through babysitting."

"WHAT ABOUT ME? WHAT ABOUT ME?" she kept screaming into the phone.

"I'll be over soon. I'm going to hang up now." And the calls started coming in, over and over.

Once, shortly after I got home from visiting her, she called me.

"Uh, Susan?"

"Hi, Mom, how are you? I was just over to visit you. Do you remember that?"

"No, you were? I don't remember. When are you coming over? We need to talk."

"I'll be over next Thursday. We can talk then."

"Where am I? We need to talk. I don't like it here. Do I have to stay here?"

"Mom, if you don't like it there, we'll start looking for another place. You don't have to stay there."

"Well, this place isn't that bad. The people are so nice here. We need to talk about it."

"Okay, when I come over on Thursday, we'll talk."

"Susan? What has happened to my house?"

By this time, I had already sold her house and divided her personal items among the family, sold them, or given them away. I didn't think it was necessary that she know, so I told her that her house and furniture were still there, safe and sound. She seemed comforted by that but was still agitated.

"Well, I want to go home."

"Mom, you have been living in this place for five months now. Do you know the address where you used to live?"

"No, where did I live?"

"The town you lived in was Elverta. Does that sound familiar?"

"No, no, it doesn't. Why can't I go home and live? Who is paying for this place?"

"The VA is paying for it," I lied again.

"Oh, we are so lucky. Dad really did right by me, didn't he?"

"Yes, he did."

We ended the call and five minutes later she called again, and again I answered. I was trying an experiment. What if I answered her call every time? Would she eventually stop? But my experiment didn't work; she didn't remember talking to me five minutes ago.

"Susan? I need a laxative. I haven't had a bowel movement in three days!"

"Mom, they give you laxatives."

"No, they don't!"

"Yes, they do."

"Well, I haven't had a bowel movement for three days! I'm going to die if I don't have a bowel movement!"

"Are you in any pain?"

"No."

"Well, I think you're going to be okay. I'll bring some laxatives to you tomorrow when I come to visit." I tried to pacify her so she would calm down.

"I need them now! I'm going to die if I don't have a bowel movement! It's been three days!"

She started to cry. I didn't know what to say or do.

"Susan? Don't get mad at me and never come visit."

"Mom, I don't care what you say or do, I will always be here for you. I will never stop visiting you."

I wondered if she was feeling guilty for getting so angry with me over this.

The next day we had the same conversation all over again. That night I went to sleep, wondering if this was ever going to end.

My mother was nothing if not persistent; she kept calling to complain that she needed a laxative until I became so frustrated with her that I finally had Sam drive all of us to a pharmacy. She was delighted and bought the strongest laxatives she thought would work. I also picked up some disposable panties for her. She was walking slowly so I stayed with her while Sam went up to the register to pay. I tapped my mother on the shoulder and pointed to Sam, who was up at the register by himself, paying for her laxatives and disposable panties.

We both doubled over laughing. It was so nice to hear her laugh, even if it was at Sam's expense.

When we got to the car, Sam turned to me and smiled. He said he told the lady at the register he was going to a party. We laughed. I discreetly opened the box of laxatives and took most of them out so my mother wouldn't overdose.

It was late when we got home, and I fell into bed exhausted. I sing in my sleep. Well actually, I hum. Sam usually wakes up and tries to name that tune. I often wake to find myself humming "Hello Again" by Neil Diamond or "I Just Called to Say I Love You" by Stevie Wonder.

I hummed these songs over and over for many months. Years later, I still find myself humming those tunes at times.

I went to visit her at least every week, sometimes two or three times in a week, and sometimes I brought her to our house to see how she reacted to spending time there with us. I found she was very anxious, and I realized that no matter where she was, she was going to feel anxious. In the end, I found it was easier, and best, to visit her at her apartment.

On one of those visits, we were sitting in her small but quaint living room. I tried talking about her past because that was the only way I knew to have a conversation with her.

We were sitting quietly when she turned to me with tears in her eyes and confided, "It's times like this that I miss your dad."

She seldom mentioned my father, so it took me by surprise. She had lived with him for 49 years and had traveled all over the world with him by her side. He had died 16 years earlier and she had become accustomed to living alone. Now she felt estranged and lonely. My eyes welled up with tears with her. I couldn't imagine what she was going through.

On June 27, 2012, I got a call at 2:00 in the morning. One of the caretakers had found her unresponsive in her bathroom and called an ambulance. She woke up, but they were required to take her to the hospital anyway. Sam and I immediately set out to the hospital emergency room and found her fully dressed and standing by the door of her room with an outraged look on her face.

"I don't know why I'm here! This is ridiculous!" she said contemptuously.

I responded, "You passed out in your room and they wanted to make sure you were okay."

"This is so ridiculous! I don't know why they made me come to this place!" She repeated this several times.

We took her back to her apartment and settled her in. A caretaker came by with her breakfast and tried to comfort her, but she was angry, and nothing calmed her down. She passed out a couple more times after that, and returned to the emergency room. I started to wonder if this was going to become a common event.

When Christmas came around, I waited until cards were mailed to her before I answered back with a note and picture of her. This was my way of telling her friends her state of mind. The note said:

> *I thought that since Mom is unable to send Christmas cards, I would do it for her and let you know what is happening to her. She no longer lives in her home, but she lives in a beautiful place and is well taken care of. I go visit her regularly and usually take her for coffee or ice cream to get her out for a while. She is doing fine but her memory has been going downhill rapidly. A year ago, she was still living alone and driving. So much has changed over this past year. Most of the time she recognizes me; although, there have been times when she doesn't, until I remind her who I am. She often asks me the names of her friends and when I tell her, she remembers them, or at least I think she does.*

Conversation is difficult because she repeats everything about every five minutes. She gets very confused and anxious and has a nervous energy, which I try to dispel by making her laugh. Sometimes I'm successful and sometimes I'm not. I try to get her to talk about her past, which she remembered vividly a month ago, but even that is starting to fade. She has lost weight, weighing about 100 pounds, but her body is like the little energizer bunny—it just keeps going and going. She refuses to use the walker, but when I take her out, she hangs onto me for dear life.

I miss my mother—especially her spunky dark sense of humor. It is torture watching her go through this and I know this is the last thing she would ever want. But it is what it is and, despite everything, every once in a while, I get to see a glimpse of the person she used to be.

Have a Merry Christmas and Happy New Year!

Susan

On one of Jim's visits, he called me, concerned that he'd seen feces all over her bathroom curtains, around the toilet, and on the floor. He was upset because not only was it unacceptable for our mother to live in such conditions, but she paid quite a lot for her care. We immediately started looking at other places. I had a good recommendation for another senior living care advisor who specialized in placing people in suitable homes, and she came out to evaluate my mother.

After visiting my mother, she told me she loved the place my mother was in and often recommended it, but that she would never have placed her there, because the place was too big for my mother, that she would continually get lost, and that it was only going to get worse. I was worried that soon she would need to be in lockdown. This wonderful woman recommended other smaller homes specifically for Alzheimer's patients. We were put on waiting lists until we finally found a beautiful home run by a man who had several around town and was known for taking good care of the residents. He interviewed us but said that he didn't accept sundowners patients. I was disappointed and worried that we might never find a suitable place for her. We told him that was what my mother was diagnosed with, but he agreed to give her a two-week trial period to see if she would fit in.

When I took my mother to the new place, I anxiously waited for her response. She stared blankly at her new environment. The owner was there to introduce himself to her and show us her room—a large room with a sliding glass door that brought in light. I told the owner that my mother was very attached to her purse and even slept with it.

Signaling with his hands he said, "Look around."

All five of the women nearby had their purses neatly tucked beside them. I laughed.

I helped my mother move in with a few items of clothing. She didn't need any furniture, so I disbursed most of it to family members. As I helped her pack, I picked up her purse. It was strangely heavy. I looked inside and found several dollars' worth of nickels. She must have taken them when they played bingo. I apologetically returned them to the first home. They laughed, stating it happened often.

A week after she moved, I was told she could stay. This home was perfect for her. It was big, beautiful, very clean, and she was never alone. She didn't have a phone to call me 20 times a day and I waited for her to say something about it, but she never did. It was like she never remembered there were phones. I think her calling was a habit, and since she had the paper with our phone numbers on it, she went down the list and called all the numbers. For the first time, I started to relax. The facility was also close to my house so I visited often.

Jim started coming Fridays and we visited her together. The women who cared for my mother were friendly and caring and welcomed us any time of the day. They always offered us a snack that they had made for the residents. They took my mother for walks every day. Once after a visit, I looked back while on my way to my car and saw the caretaker with her arm wrapped in my mother's. I felt a pang when I saw the vacant look in my mother's eyes and cried on the way home. *God, never let me go through this! Never let me put my children through this!*

One day I spontaneously took my mother to a nearby café for coffee. When we arrived, I noticed that she was anxious and looking nervously around. I thought back to the time when she would have been comfortable and confident, and now she seemed small and helpless and unsure of herself. I decided to take her over and get her settled before going to the counter and ordering our coffee. I knew her anxiousness was a symptom of Alzheimer's disease, but I still wasn't prepared for my strong, independent mother to react this way.

Often when I visited, my mother would ask, "Susan? Where are my rings?"

I always answered, "They are in my safe deposit box at the bank,"

"Well, the next time you come visit will you bring them to me?"

"Yes, I will," I answered. She had lost so much weight they wouldn't stay on her fingers and I wasn't going to risk her losing them. A thought occurred to me that I could have a ring that looked like hers made of zirconia instead of real diamonds, but I never got around to it.

One beautiful sunny day, I went to visit and walked in to find my mother in the senior home's kitchen. I could only imagine how she was trying to help them, as she used to do with me. The caretakers found little tasks for her to do so she wouldn't bother them while they cooked.

She recognized me and said, "Susan! I remember."

"What do you remember, Mom?"

"I remember everything! I remember everything!"

I immediately panicked. I felt a hot sensation creep up my face and my breathing became labored. What if there had been a blood clot on her brain and she was fine now? I had sold her house and disposed of all her belongings. She would be furious with me. I started frantically thinking of what I should do. She would have to come live with me. My heart was pounding. I felt a cold sweat slowly envelop me.

Hoarsely I choked, "Let's go sit down and talk about this."

We settled on the living room couch, where I started questioning her.

"Where do you live?"

"I don't remember. Where do I live?"

I started to breathe again. Even though I would have given anything for her to remember and become her normal self again, part of me was relieved that I didn't have to explain what I had done.

As I left her at the dinner table, I heard her exclaim to anybody who would listen, "I remember! I remember everything!"

Thirteen months after her diagnosis, Jim and I went to visit her. Her mind was still rapidly declining. The doctors told me that once a mind started rapidly declining, it would continue to do so. I wondered how much longer she would be able to communicate. Jim and I sat on the couch with her in between us. I asked her if she remembered the time I dated a pilot. With vacant eyes, she nodded yes, but I seriously doubted it. I told the story of how he teased me about becoming his copilot of a DC-4 airplane. I got in and sat in the copilot's seat, but couldn't see out the windshield, nor reach the pedals with my feet. I looked over at him and asked if he still wanted me to be his copilot. It was mainly small talk to help pass the time, but to my surprise my mother threw her hands up to her face and started belly laughing. It was one of those contagious heartfelt laughs of hers that I so loved. We all started laughing. It was a moment I treasure and wished there had been more of.

I went to visit on one of my regularly scheduled days, and again my mother was in the kitchen "helping" the caretakers cook. I took her into the living room so we could have some privacy.

She became very agitated, grabbing my arm and screaming, "Where's the baby? Where's the baby?"

I had no idea what she was talking about.

"What baby?" I asked.

She screamed, "The baby. I'm supposed to take care of the baby. It's outside!"

I started frantically thinking for a way to calm her down.

"Mom, the baby is with his daddy."

That seemed to work, and with a relieved sigh she said, "Oh, that is good news."

A few minutes later she screamed, "Where's the baby?"

Without hesitation, I exclaimed, "The baby is with his daddy."

"Oh, that is good news."

This conversation repeated several more times.

Sometimes when I visited around lunch, I sat at the table and joined them. The caretakers always tried to include Jim and me whenever we visited. My mother seemed content that we were there.

On one of my visits, my mother looked over at me and said, "Every morning when I wake up, I don't know where I am, and I'm so scared."

Tears came to my eyes and I felt my stomach drop. Did I do the wrong thing? Should I have found a way for her to live in her home? Should I have brought her into my home? I knew that many people with Alzheimer's felt this way even in their own homes, but somehow this didn't comfort me.

The caretakers were wonderful women and did everything they could to make me feel comfortable. They laughingly admitted to me that when my mother first arrived, she sometimes jerked the curtains down from her bedroom window, stuffed washcloths down the toilet, and tried to get away from them when they attempted to stop her. They felt like she was taunting them by looking back over her shoulder and crying out, "Catch me if you can!"

My mother never wrote anything in cards and she never wrote me letters. She always signed the cards she gave me, "Love and prayers, Mom." So I don't have many writings from her. I found an old address book of hers and upon opening it I noticed a quote in her handwriting.

>Faith is a gift.
>It's a hope and a prayer.
>It's trusting in God,
>And it's knowing he is there.
>
>Truth is a gift.
>It's a hope and a prayer.
>It's trusting in God,
>And knowing he is there.

Just having something in her handwriting is precious. All the names and addresses are also in her handwriting. I will treasure this old address book forever.

CHAPTER 22

Her Final Days

"It's Susan. I don't know which one they want me to press here so I pressed them all. I'm calling [my phone number]. I don't know where you are but that is where I am so give me a call."

* * *

In January 2013, my mother was taken to the emergency room and diagnosed with aspiration pneumonia and a urinary tract infection. Because they didn't think she would survive another six months, she qualified for hospice. By now she was very thin and weak. She still refused to use her walker. Instead, she clutched someone's arm for balance.

When Sam and I visited her, we both noticed how rapidly her mind was deteriorating. I left Sam alone with her while I went to the bathroom.

Out of his own curiosity, Sam took the opportunity to ask, "What really happened between Sue and your brother?"

I had told Sam about my uncle molesting me and he wanted to gauge her reaction.

Suddenly her eyes widened in surprise, "You know? Susan knows."

And then just as suddenly she faded back into emptiness.

The home where my mother lived rarely called me, so I was alarmed when I received a call from them. They explained they had to rush her to the emergency room when she jerked away from one of the caretakers and fell, hitting her head hard on the floor.

When I arrived at the hospital, the doctor took me aside and said she had broken three bones in her face and around the left eye, and that there was a hemorrhage in her brain that normally would require surgery. He continued, explaining that he didn't think she would survive surgery and said it would be too traumatic for her if they tried, so with the help of the caretakers, we took her back to the home with morphine.

When we got there, the caretaker who tried to catch her was sobbing, "It was all my fault."

I went over and took her in my arms, whispering in her ear, "It was an accident."

She looked up at me with appreciative tears in her eyes.

We tried to settle my mother into the deluxe recliner next to her bed, but she kept squirming and trying to throw her legs over the side. I'm not sure if it was the morphine, her sundowners, or both that caused her to struggle against us. I finally stepped back, looked at the caretaker who was trying to help me, and shrugged. We let my mother squirm for a while until we were satisfied that she couldn't get herself out of the chair. At one point I knelt down and took both of her hands in mine.

Hoarsely she whispered, "This sucks!"

I sympathized, "I'm so sorry, this must really suck!"

"Yes, this really sucks!"

Those were the last words she spoke out loud.

She was still on hospice, but the caretakers of the home took care of her needs. In all the excitement, they forgot to call hospice before rushing her to the hospital. I'm sure they wanted to get her emergency attention immediately. According to hospice and my mother's insurance, the caretakers were supposed to call hospice before taking her to the hospital. As a result, I got statements from Medicare and her government insurance, Tricare, for months after her death, showing the denial of insurance coverage that normally would have paid for her hospital expenses. I kept waiting for the bill from the hospital. Instead, each time I received the Medicare and Tricare statements, the expenses had been exponentially lowered until the hospital finally absorbed the cost and my mother was never billed.

The caretakers thought she would probably live a couple of weeks. She died one week later. It was just enough time for the family to come and say their goodbyes.

I spent the entire Sunday before she died reading to her from a novel I had started. I don't remember what the novel was about, I just hoped she might be able to hear my voice. I got to a part of the book that explicitly described sex between a man and woman. I stopped, scrolled down the page, and told her we would skip over that section, though knowing my mother, she probably would have wanted me to read the passage to her.

On Monday, May 20, 2013, I decided to go to work while Jim and Christy stayed with her throughout the day. They went home that evening, just before I went to see her. When I got there, I started the walk down the long familiar hallway toward her room, delayed a bit while each caretaker gave me a long, warm hug and predicted she would only live another day or two. As I stepped into her room, I noticed her breathing was labored and her eyes were open in glassy slits. She still wasn't coherent, and when I saw her, I desperately wanted to turn and run. Instead, I took a deep breath and walked into her room.

Holding back tears I managed to say, "Mom, it's time for you to go. You aren't living life. This isn't living. Everybody has said their goodbyes and told you they love you. I love you. Dad is waiting for you up there. Edith and Bill are waiting for you up there."

I started to tell her that she and Edith could create all kinds of hell up there but decided better of it and instead said, "You and Edith could create all kinds of trouble up there."

Not knowing what else to say, I sat down next to her. I was numb and despondent.

After some time had passed, I heard my mother's voice asking, "Susan! How do I die?"

I looked up, but she was expressionless and hadn't moved from her comatose position. I sat silently for a moment, just looking at her.

I thought, rather than said, to her, *Take a deep breath and after you exhale, don't breathe back in.*

As I sat watching her, she took a deep breath in and slowly exhaled. I waited for her to inhale again but the inhale never happened. There was no death rattle, no struggle. I waited. Nothing. She was gone.

ACKNOWLEDGMENTS

I must start by thanking my awesome husband, Sam, who read many drafts and inspired confidence and insight with an unwavering devotion.

I am grateful to my children, Rebekah, Matt, and Amanda who not only expressed an enthusiastic interest but also are an integral part of this book, I would not have been able to tell this story without the richness they have brought to my life.

I am especially grateful to to my brother Jim for his constant encouragement and support.

A special thanks to my friend Kris Harper, who devotedly read through and edited many early drafts. She stood by me through my struggles and gave me encouragement when I almost gave up. That is true friendship.

Writing a book about my life was a surreal process. I'm forever indebted to Elizabeth deNoma and Maura McGurk for their editorial help, insightful suggestions, and support in bringing my story to life. Their sensitivity inspired confidence and encouraged excellence. They not only helped me with the structure of paragraphs and sentences but also with their enthusiastic comments that emboldened me to go forward. It is because of their efforts and encouragement that I have a legacy to pass on to my family.

Susan Morley, born in a military hospital in Shirley, Massachusetts, came to California when she was 12. She worked over 30 years in the California court system and graduated from University of San Francisco. She and her husband love to travel, hike, cook, drink good wine, and spend time with family and friends. They live in El Dorado Hills, California.

www.ingramcontent.com/pod-product-compliance
Lightning Source LLC
Chambersburg PA
CBHW072223200426
43209CB00073B/1927/J